READING CHAUCER'S POEMS

Reading

CHAUCER'S POEMS

A GUIDED SELECTION BY

Bernard O'Donoghue

FABER & FABER

First published in 2015
by Faber & Faber Ltd
Bloomsbury House
74–77 Great Russell Street
London WC1B 3DA

Typeset by RefineCatch Ltd
Printed and bound in England by CPI Group (UK) Ltd, Croydon, CR0 4YY

A CIP record for this book is available from the British Library

ISBN 978–0–571–23065–5

FSC
www.fsc.org
MIX
Paper from
responsible sources
FSC® C101712

2 4 6 8 10 9 7 5 3 1

Contents

~

Introduction   VII
Chronology   XXI

The Book of the Duchess (*c.*1368)   3
The House of Fame (*c.*1379)   13
The Parliament of Fowls (early 1380s?)   25
Troilus and Criseyde (mid-1380s?)   53
Chaucers Wordes Unto Adam, His Owne Scriveyn
    (mid/late 1380s?)   117
The Legend of Good Women (1386–7?)   119
Truth: Balade de Bon Conseyl (late 1380s?)   135
Lak of Stedfastnesse (late 1390s?)   139
Lenvoy de Chaucer a Scogan (1390s?)   143

V

The Canterbury Tales (*c*.1388–1400)   147
   General Prologue   148
      The Knight   150
      The Prioress   152
      The Monk   155
      The Clerk of Oxford   156
      The Franklin   157
      The Wife of Bath   158
      The Reeve   159
      The Summoner   160
      The Pardoner   161
      The Author makes his excuses   162
   The Knight's Tale   164
   The Miller's Tale   172
   The Wife of Bath's Prologue   178
   The Pardoner's Tale   187
   The Merchant's Prologue   200
   The Nun's Priest's Tale   203
   The Canon's Yeoman's Prologue and Tale   212
   The Manciple's Tale   217
   'The Retractions', wherein 'Taketh the makere of this
      book his leve'   221
The Complaint of Chaucer to His Purse   223

Introduction

∾

Given how little we know about the lives of any of his predecessors in English poetry, it is remarkable how much we do know about Chaucer. He grew up in London and lived there all his life, apart from professional trips to France, Spain, Italy and to other parts of England. His family was well off: his grandfather was a wine merchant from Ipswich who moved to London to set up the business into which his son, Geoffrey's father, succeeded him. Little is known about the education of the poet, who was an only child; despite the impressive erudition and love of learning evident throughout his writings, he seems not to have gone to university. He was a prominent courtier and civil servant, starting out in his early teens as a page in the service of the Countess of Ulster, and by 1360 serving in the retinue of her husband Lionel Duke of Clarence in a bloody period during the Hundred Years War in France. He was captured at a battle near Rheims, and ransomed, the tradition is, by the king, Edward III. In 1367 he married Philippa de Roet, the daughter of a Flemish knight and probably the sister of Katherine

Swynford, the mistress and ultimately third wife of Edward III's powerful and dictatorial son, John of Gaunt, Duke of Lancaster. It was the connections with Gaunt in particular that kept Chaucer prominent in public affairs.

Though Chaucer probably translated parts of *Le Roman de la Rose* (the Middle English verse version, *The Romaunt of the Rose*, which is half-heartedly included at the end of all modern editions of Chaucer, is possibly his) and wrote short poems in French and English in the 1360s, his first major poem was *The Book of the Duchess*, probably written as an elegy for the death of Gaunt's first wife Blanche (the mother of Henry IV) in 1368. Thereafter Chaucer was an active public servant and writer, though the sequence of events is not always clear. It is possible, though the evidence is not wholly conclusive, that Chaucer travelled to Italy and Ireland in Lionel's entourage. He certainly visited Genoa on trade missions in 1372 and 1373. The public and literary activities sometimes co-incided: for example, it was probably on a diplomatic trip to Lombardy that he encountered the works of Boccaccio, at least two of which he drew on for major works, *The Knight's Tale* and *Troilus and Criseyde*. His roles in public life were significant: he was a Justice of the Peace, and in 1386 a Knight of the Shire for Kent, in which capacity he was a member of the 'Wonderful Parliament' in October and November 1386 which marked an important escalation of the hostilities between the young king and parliament. In the mid-1380s he composed *Troilus and Criseyde*, and he was engaged on his most famous work, *The Canterbury Tales*, from the late 1380s until his death in 1400. There is no record of the date or circumstances of his death, despite the amusing and lurid speculations in Terry Jones's whodunnit *Who Murdered Chaucer? A Medieval Mystery* (2003).

The first striking quality of Chaucer's writing is its capacity to express general truths. We immediately recognise the world he creates. This is not the quality that our era most prizes in poetry though. In his first 'Milton' essay, T. S. Eliot criticises the imagery of 'L'Allegro' and 'Il Penseroso' for being 'all general'. He objects to the lines about the ploughman 'who whistles o'er the furrowed land' and the milkmaid who 'singeth blithe' that 'it is not a particular ploughman, milkmaid and shepherd . . . (as Wordsworth might see them)', but an aural effect 'joined to the concepts of ploughman, milkmaid, and shepherd'. On these principles, he would not like Chaucer (and indeed Eliot, unlike Ezra Pound who said that 'Chaucer had a deeper knowledge of life than Shakespeare', has little to say about him). When he is most serious, Chaucer, of whom Dryden in the preface to his *Fables* concluded 'here is God's plenty', has a penchant for the general truth and the perfect cameo to represent it: 'the smylere with the knyf under the cloke' amongst the horrific depictions on the walls of the Temple of Mars in *The Knight's Tale*; the plight of Criseyde 'with women fewe among the Grekis stronge'; the insights about writing in the introduction to his classical dream-poem *The Legend of Good Women*:

And yf that olde bokes were aweye	*books had been lost*
Yloren were of remembraunce the keye.	*Lost*

This kind of generalising power is not what we have looked for in poetry since Eliot and the modernists. Chaucer shares with Dickens and Jane Austen the capacity to create a character – or caricature – with a telling stroke of the pen: the Medical Doctor on the Canterbury pilgrimage who 'knew the cause of every malady' and, recognising that 'gold in physic is a cordial, therefore . . . lovede gold in special'. Nowhere was there anyone as busy as the Lawyer on the pilgrimage: 'and yet he semed bisier than he was.' We recognise these vocational clichés, and admire the *mot juste* in their expression.

Chaucer is of course a great entertainer, as everyone knows. As well as generalities, there are cameos of more particular wit and astuteness: the presumptuous monk in *The Friar's Tale* who takes over the house he visits, 'and fro the bench he drove away the cat'; the exuberance of *The Miller's Tale* in Alysoun's exclamation after she has pulled in from the window 'hir naked ers':

> 'Tehee!' quod she, and clapte the wyndow to.

As an entertaining presence, the Wife of Bath manifests both tendencies, enlivening her general traits – mostly the stereotypical details of the shrewish wife – with vivid verbal details, addressing one of her wretched husbands as 'old barrelful of lies' and bursting out with the great lament –

> Allas, Allas! That evere love was synne!

Yet none of this – generalising power or sparkling verbal cameos – would establish Chaucer as one of the greatest poets in English. He would still be open to the reservation which Matthew Arnold appended to his admiration of him: that he lacks 'high seriousness', one of 'the grand virtues of poetry'. But something else, less obvious and less generally noticed, does make Chaucer's poetic gift extraordinary. In a few brilliant pages of *Seven Types of Ambiguity* William Empson anatomises an extract from *Troilus and Criseyde*, showing that it has the same verbal density and ironies of language as the most accomplished lyric. Empson states the problem for the narrative poet acutely, illustrating in passing perhaps why our era is unreceptive to the long poem. 'In a long narrative poem the stress on particular phrases must be slight, most of the lines do not expect more attention than you would give to phrases of a novel when reading it aloud; you would not look for the same concentration of imagery as in a lyric. On the other hand, a long poem accumulates imagery.'

But Empson goes on to show how Chaucer's poetry, as well as accumulating a sustained imagery, *does* respond remarkably well to the kind of attention you would give to a lyric. Let me give a few examples (most from texts which are included in this selection) of Chaucer's skill with imagery, from the work that stands with *Troilus and Criseyde* as his greatest: *The Canterbury Tales*. The first is the most bizarre episode in the whole journey to Canterbury: the extraordinary appearance of the Canon and his Yeoman. If Chaucer had seriously planned to complete the ambitious programme of the *Tales* – to write four stories each for thirty-odd pilgrims – he hardly helped his cause by introducing two more characters, the mysterious Canon and his attendant Yeoman, a few miles from the end of the pilgrimage. Would this require eight more tales? The episode begins with one of Chaucer's memorably exuberant lines: as the fat Canon comes galloping on a hot day to catch up with the pilgrims, he is sweating 'that it wonder was to see'; he (or possibly his horse) is so flecked with sweaty foam that he looks as two-toned as a magpie:

> But it was joye for to seen hym swete!

So far so amusing! But this Canon is a very strange figure: an alchemist as it turns out (anticipating the comedy of Ben Jonson: a dramatist whose work Chaucer's resembles in the mixture of the general and the particular I have been noting). In the first 26 lines of the Canon's Yeoman's Prologue, sweat is mentioned four times and the foam of sweat twice. The Canon's forehead, we are told, drips like 'a stillatorie' – a vessel or room for distillation. In short, this alchemist is presented as a personified still. And when the Canon overhears what his Yeoman is going to talk about, 'he fledde awey for verray sorwe and shame' and we hear no more about him. He is as evanescent as the Cheshire Cat – as deliquescent as the materials of his absurd and sinister art. The story that follows, *The Canon's Yeoman's Tale*, is an account of the machinations of the alchemists, sustained and held together by a language drenched with liquid and sublimation: the 'spirites ascencioun' from the pot and glasses, the urinals and descensories, waters rubifying and bulls' gall, water's albification, dung and piss and imbibing, fermentation and corrosive waters. Throughout the description the alchemist is shown sweating as he labours over the fire; at the end Plato (amongst the philosophers that speak 'mistily') expounds how water is made of four elements but will not say what they are. It is, the narrator concludes, the fiend's work, represented by this *tour de force* of liquidity. It is a good illustration of Empson's praise of the Chaucerian long poem building by accumulating and densening imagery.

In the same way, the Prologue and Tale of the loathsome Pardoner are suffused with disgust at man's physical nature, expressed as a sacrilegious variant of doctrinal truth, a parody of the Eucharist (echoing Joyce for the modernist reader). The Pardoner says his 'theme' is always the same: that cupidity is the root of all evils. One form of it is the greed for food and drink: even Swift can not surpass the Pardoner's loathing for bodily operations (a loathing which he attributes to St Paul):

> O wombe! O bely! O stynkyng cod,   *stomach; codpiece*
> Fulfilled of dong and of corrupcioun!   *full of shit*

At either ende of thee foul is the soun . . .   *sound*
Thise cookes, how they stampe, and streyne, and grynde,
                                                    pound and strain
And turnen substaunce into accident
To fulfille al thy likerous talent.   *your gluttonous demands*

There is nothing so philosophical and blasphemously brilliant in St
Paul as the extraordinary turning of 'substaunce into accident' here:
the Christian understanding of the Eucharist is to see beyond the
accidental into the underlying divine substaunce, the 'Real Presence'.
The Pardoner's chefs take the material substance of food – the
material which was hunted laboriously from 'est and west and north
and south, / In erthe, in eir, in water' – and reduce it to insubstantial
dishes for the gourmet. They make presence *un*real. It is an astonish-
ing image, and one which powerfully sets up the world of destructive
and irresponsible corruption in the following tale told by the
Pardoner, the greatest short story in early English literature. Wilson
Knight's luminous observation that a Shakespeare play is like an
extended metaphor because of the way it sustains and deepens its
central image applies exactly to this skill in Chaucer, found in many
places beyond these two examples. As in Shakespeare, we don't
notice it happening. There is no poet in English – comparison might
be made with the Metaphysicals, or with the writers of 'Philosophic
Words' in the eighteenth century – that carries so much learning so
lightly and within such a crucible of imagery as Chaucer: no poet
who is such a brilliant dramatist.

But the fact remains that Chaucer is, first and last, a narrative
writer: his units are extensive, as Empson says. Since Dryden first
called him 'the father of English poetry' at the end of the seventeenth
century it has always been found difficult to present him in manage-
able extracts in his original language to his modern readers.

Moreover, his fourteenth-century language is not very easy to understand (though not as difficult as that of many of his contemporaries, or as difficult as one might expect of a writer two hundred years earlier than Shakespeare: his language is sometimes easier than Shakespeare's Elizabethan eloquence, the 'Othello music'). The most successful recent anthology was Nevill Coghill's 1961 selections for Faber, made readable by the unusual strategy of having the texts faced by the modern verse versions which Coghill did so well (he called them 'paraphrases', even though they extended to about three-quarters of the length of the originals most of the time).

Of course the biggest difficulty in making selections is deciding how to represent *The Canterbury Tales*, one of the very greatest long works in English and one with a powerful coherence to it, despite its unfinished and fragmentary form, and its generic variety. Most tales are too long to represent in their entirety; here I have included only *The Pardoner's Tale* more or less in full – nothing gives a more complete sense of Chaucer's narrative drive and thematic cogency. Some set pieces are unforgettable but too *short* to include as an extract, such as the wonderfully frosty, Brueghel-like cameo from *The Franklin's Tale*:

> The bittre frostes, with the sleet and reyn,
> Destroyed hath the grene in every yerd.   *yard*
> Janus sit by the fyr, with double berd,
> And drynketh of his bugle horn the wyn;
> Biforn hym stant brawen of the tusked swyn,   *meat; boar*
> And 'Nowel' crieth every lusty man.   *Noel!*

This passage comes the morning after an evening in the company of a magician, whose spells and their end inevitably bring to mind Prospero's cloud-capped towers and revels in *The Tempest*:

And whan this maister that this magyk wroughte   *scholar*
Saugh it was tyme, he clapte his hands two,
And farewel! Al oure revele was ago.   *entertainment*
And yet remoeved they nevere out of the hous,
Whil they saugh al this sighte merveillous,
But in his studie, ther as his bookes be,
They seten stille, and no wight but they thre.

As ever, of course, I hope that these samples will tempt the reader to proceed further into the pages of the Riverside Edition: the nine hundred lines of *The Franklin's Tale* are too long for inclusion here, but the tale's haunting magic and writerly elegance would be a good text to go on to.

There is another difficulty in offering Chaucer to a modern readership: one, though, which is more solvable than we might expect, and which this selection attempts to redress. Because of the pre-eminence of *The Canterbury Tales* in Chaucer's corpus, most modern editions begin with that and its familiar opening lines about April's soft showers, even though the *Tales* were his maturest work. This opening of the *General Prologue* is a hard act to follow. But we know enough about Chaucer's life (much more than we know about Shakespeare, for example), both from his own testimony and because he was a public servant, to give a rough chronology of his writing life and to order the works accordingly.

The chronological order is important, not just for its scholarly interest, but because Chaucer's style and literary manner changed and – it is fair to claim – matured throughout his writing life. At the risk of over-simplifying, his early works were influenced by French literary traditions (we know that Chaucer himself wrote in French, though we cannot identify with certainty any surviving French works as his); his middle-period writing was influenced by his great Italian predecessors and earlier contemporaries Boccaccio and Petrarch; and his latest writings, such as the later *Canterbury Tales*, had their own style, compounded of French and native English, drawing on all those predecessors and the whole post-classical tradition he was heir to. It is this mature complex style and literary attitude that provide the securest grounds for claiming for Chaucer the status of founding father of English literature. (C. S. Lewis said memorably that the whole mixed style of subsequent English poetry is found in seed in Chaucer's beautifully balanced line 'Singest with vois memorial in the shade' from the strange minor poem *Anelida and Arcite*: the Old English-derived 'singest' and 'shade' wrapped round the French 'vois' and 'memorial', in a combination of English and French word-order.)

Some of the dates given here are speculative (particularly with some of the short poems, like 'Truth'), and parts of *The Canterbury Tales* predate the general placing of that work after 1388 (for example, Chaucer had probably translated *The Knight's Tale* from Boccaccio's *Teseida* at least as early as the early 1380s); but I have tried to keep to a plausible order so that these selections give an impression of the poet's development. We begin with the French-derived octosyllabics of *The Book of the Duchess*, almost certainly written for the death in about 1368 of Blanche of Lancaster, the wife of Chaucer's patron, John of Gaunt, who was the brother-in-law of the poet's wife. And, with one exception, we end with the 'Retraction' at the end of the *Tales*: not that I want to suggest that this was written, like Yeats's last poems, on the poet's deathbed as was implausibly suggested a generation ago by a sympathetic reader of Chaucer, John Gardner, but because it offers a logical coda to Chaucer's last and most substantial work. The exception is 'The Complaint of Chaucer to His

Purse', a poem which ends with an 'envoy' (letter) to the new king Henry IV, which means that its writing must be very close to Chaucer's death in about 1400. It also makes a spirited conclusion to the writings: an urbane and half-humorous complaint in Chaucer's most accomplished mature style and in the seven-line rhyme royal stanza that he used for many of his major works.

So where, finally, can the appeal of Chaucer for a modern reader be most reliably found? It has proved difficult for professional criticism to agree about exactly where his strengths lie, for reasons touched on at the start of this introduction. Critical approaches have tended to emanate from one of two extreme positions: either 'the good old Chaucer' school which sees the poet as an entertainer – something like what he himself calls a 'tregetour', a 'sleight-of-hand artist' as the Riverside Edition glosses it; or an exegetical school which shows him, accurately enough, as a learned, bookish author of the late Middle Ages – a figure parodied by Chaucer himself when the eagle in *The House of Fame* rebukes him for going home to his house where as 'domb (*dumb*) as any stoon, / Thou sittest at another book / Tyl fully daswed (*dazed*) is thy look': dazed from reading. Chaucer's fondness for learning is most touchingly evident in his ideal portrait of the Clerk of Oxford in the *General Prologue*: a man too unworldly to have a clerical benefice (in contrast to the bitterly unfulfilled ambitious clergymen of a century later, Skelton and Dunbar), a man who would rather have at his bed's head

> Twenty bookes, clad in blak or reed,   *bound*
> Of Aristotle and his philosophie,
> Than robes riche, or fithele, or gay sautrie.   *fiddles; psaltery*

One of his greatest and most attractive works, *The Nun's Priest's Tale*, incorporates a complex weave of classical learning into an innocent, plain-style mock-heroic fable about 'a fox, or of a cok and hen'. Besides, like the other major poets of learning in the Middle Ages (the greatest, of course, is Dante), Chaucer is also a profound love poet, and not only because the tradition in which he wrote was the heritage of Ovid and the medieval love poets, from the Troubadours to Dante and from the great German epics of love to the romance-writers of the Renaissance. Chaucer, like his creation Pandarus, had his own 'feeling' for love (though, like Pandarus, he denied that he had it). It is evident all over his writings, from the endless eloquent evocations of the folly of love to Criseyde's head-spinning reaction to Troilus riding by – 'Who yaf me drynke?'

In the end the critical dilemma is rather as with rebutting Tolstoy's attack on Shakespeare: it is easier to recognise and illustrate the excellence of Chaucer than to characterise it definitively. One thing we can say at least is that criticism has in several eras not served Chaucer well. For example, when originality was prized above all else, it seemed a flaw that Chaucer's stories (like Shakespeare's) were copies or translations of earlier works. When it was shown that the figures in the *General Prologue* to *The Canterbury Tales* were types or copies rather than new creations, it was felt to be a diminution of Chaucer's greatness. Chaucer's Wife of Bath is closely modelled on 'La Vieille', the old lady who protects the rosebud in *The Romaunt of the Rose* (herself a formidable and compelling creation); but that is not to say she is not an irresistible creature when she laments 'Allas, Allas! That evere love was synne!' A poetics that deals conclusively with the great writers that took their inspiration from predecessors rather than reality – writers like Virgil, Dante, Chaucer and Shakespeare – has never quite been found. Criticism seems fated to wander off on its own beat. With Chaucer it often warns us about anachronism – for example in finding proto-feminist elements in him, long *avant la lettre*, it might seem. But we might counter that Gavin Douglas, not much more than a century after Chaucer, declared him to be 'ever all women's friend'.

I hope that Chaucer's various appeals are represented here: his narrative compulsion; his keen-eyed wit; an unsurpassed vividness of characterisation and linguistic depth. You find yourself repeatedly reaching out towards the descendants of this father of English literature: to Ben Jonson or Shakespeare or Pope or the novelists of general wit – Austen or above all Dickens. It may be that we are too influenced by that later heritage to give full value to the religious side of Chaucer's writing; the 'plenty' that Dryden found in him has many aspects. But we inevitably feel now that it is not just the language of English literature which is germinating in Chaucer: it is the typical and most humorous concerns of that literature itself.

Chronology

Late 1330s	Boccaccio's *Il Filostrato* (principal source of Chaucer's Troilus)
1337	Start of the Hundred Years War with France
1339–42	Boccaccio's *Teseida* (source of Chaucer's *Knight's Tale*)
Early 1340s	Geoffrey Chaucer born in London
Early 1350s	Boccaccio's *Decameron*: some stories in common with *The Canterbury Tales*
1357	Chaucer a page in the household of the Countess of Ulster, Wife of Prince Lionel, son of Edward III
1359–60	Chaucer captured and ransomed while serving in the company of Prince Lionel in Northern France
1366	Chaucer on a diplomatic mission in Navarre; Chaucer's father dies and his mother marries again; Chaucer marries Philippa de Roet
*c.*1368	*The Book of the Duchess* (written perhaps soon after the death of Blanche, Duchess of Lancaster and wife of John of Gaunt)
1372–3	Chaucer on diplomatic mission to Italy (Florence and Genoa)

1374	Chaucer made controller of customs in the port of London: lives above the gate of Aldgate
1377	Death of Edward III, succeeded by his eleven-year-old grandson Richard II, son of the Black Prince (who died the previous year); Chaucer on missions to France
1378	Start of Great Western Schism in the Church: two popes; Chaucer on mission to Lombardy
1379–80?	*The House of Fame*
1381	Richard II marries Anne of Bohemia
Early 1380s	*The Parliament of Fowls*
Mid-1380s	*Troilus and Criseyde*
1386	Chaucer briefly MP for Kent
1386–8	Series of contentious parliaments, curbing the power of Richard II; Chaucer's connection John of Gaunt a major power
1386–7	*The Legend of Good Women*
1387	Death of Chaucer's wife Philippa
1389	Strengthening of Richard II's power; Chaucer made Clerk of the King's Works, a role from which he resigns in 1391
Late 1380s	Beginning of *The Canterbury Tales*, on which Chaucer works (along with parts of *The Legend of Good Women* and some shorter poems) for the rest of his life
1399	Death of John of Gaunt; his son Henry of Lancaster deposes and murders Richard II, and rules as Henry IV; Chaucer lives near the Lady Chapel of Westminster Abbey (24 December)
1400	Death of Chaucer, perhaps on 25 October

READING CHAUCER'S POEMS

The Book of the Duchess

∾

This poem is generally agreed to be the earliest of Chaucer's definitely assigned works, dated to *c.*1368 and thought to be an elegy for Blanche of Lancaster, the wife of John of Gaunt, Chaucer's patron and his wife's brother-in-law. It is quite closely based on French predecessor vision-poems. These are the opening lines: the insomniac (lovelorn?) poet starts reading.

> I have gret wonder, be this lyght,
> How that I lyve, for day ne nyght
> I may nat slepe wel nygh noght;
> I have so many an ydel thoght
> Purely for defaute of slep,
> That, by my trouthe, I take no kep
> Of nothing, how hit cometh or gooth,
> Ne me nys nothyng leef nor looth.
> Al is ylyche good to me –

Joye or sorowe, wherso hyt be –   10
For I have felynge in nothyng,
But as yt were a mased thyng,
Alway in poynt to falle a-doun;
For sorwful ymaginacioun
Ys alway hooly in my mynde.
  And wel ye woot, agaynes kynde
Hyt were to lyven in thys wyse;
For nature wolde nat suffyse
To noon erthly creature
Nat longe tyme to endure   20
Withoute slep and be in sorwe.
And I ne may, ne nyght ne morwe,
Slepe; and thus melancolye
And drede I have for to dye.
Defaute of slep and hevynesse
Hath sleyn my spirit of quyknesse,
That I have lost al lustyhede.
Suche fantasies ben in myn hede
So I not what is best to doo.

1–9 (overleaf): may nat] *cannot*   defaute] *lack*   take no] *don't care about*
leef nor looth] *good or bad*   ylyche] *equally*
10–19: wherso] *wherever*   felynge] *sense*   mased] *dazed*   in poynt] *on the point
of*   kynde] *nature*
20–9: hevynesse] *depression*   quyknesse] *liveliness*   That] *so that*
lustyhede] *animation*

But men myght axe me why soo   30
I may not sleepe, and what me is?
But natheles, who aske this
Leseth his asking trewely.
Myselven can not telle why
The sothe; but trewly, as I gesse,
I holde hit be a sicknesse
That I have suffred this eight yeer;
And yet my boote is never the ner,
For there is phisicien but oon
That may me hele; but that is don.   40
Passe we over untill eft;
That wil not be mot nede be left;
Our first mater is good to kepe.
  So when I saw I might not slepe
Til, now late, this other night
Upon my bed I sat upright
And bad oon reche me a book,
A romaunce, and he it me tok
To rede and drive the night away;

30–9: what me is] *what is the matter with me*   Leseth his asking] *wastes his time asking*   gesse] *suppose*   holde] *think*   boote] *cure*   ner] *nearer*
but oon] *only one*
40–9: hele] *cure*   eft] *later*   mot nede be left] *must be done without*
mater] *subject*   Til] *until*   late] *recently*   oon] *somebody*   drive] *pass*

For me thoughte it better play   50
Then play either at ches or tables
  And in this bok were written fables
That clerkes had in olde tyme,
And other poets, put in rime
To rede, and for to be in minde
While men loved the lawe of kinde.
This bok ne spak but of such thinges,
Of quenes lives, and of kinges,
And many other thinges smale.
Amonge al this I fond a tale   60
That me thoughte a wonder thing.

The dreamer reads the story of Ceyx and Alcyone, and how Alcyone, kept awake by worry about her absent husband, discovers his fate by enlisting the help of Morpheus, the god of dreams. The dreamer successfully does the same and has a strange dream in which a puppy, on the fringes of a hunt, leads him to a Man in Black, a young courtly lover, who is lamenting his wife's death (interpreted as John of Gaunt lamenting for his dead duchess). But the narrative oddness of the development is more remarkable than the poem's elegiac qualities.

50–61: play] *entertainment*   ches] *chess*   tables] *backgammon*   fables] *stories*
be in minde] *recall*   the lawe of kinde] *the law of Nature*   smale] *lesser*

6

In the following passage (387ff), the dreamer, walking towards a tree in his dream to watch a hunt, encounters the little dog.

> I was go walked fro my tree,
> And as I wente, ther cam by mee
> A whelp, that fauned me as I stood,
> That hadde yfolowed, and koude no good.   390
> Hyt com and crepte to me as lowe,
> Ryght as hyt hadde me yknowe,
> Helde doun hys hed and joyned hys eres,
> And leyde al smothe doun hys heres.
> I wolde have kaught hyt, and anoon
> Hyt fledde and was fro me goon;
> And I hym folwed, and hyt forth wente
> Doun by a floury grene wente
> Ful thikke of gras, ful softe and swete,
> With floures fele, faire under fete,   400
> And litel used, hyt semed thus;
> For bothe Flora and Zephirus,
> They two that make floures growe,

387-9: by mee] *up to me*   fauned me] *fawned on me*
390-9: koude no good] *didn't know what to do*   heres] *hair*   wente] *path*
400-3: fele] *many*   Zephirus] *the West Wind*

7

Had mad her dwellynge ther, I trowe;
For hit was, on to beholde,
As thogh the erthe envye wolde
To be gayer than the heven,
To have moo floures, swiche seven,
As in the welken sterres bee.
Hyt had forgete the povertee   410
That wynter, through his colde morwes,
Had mad hit suffre, and his sorwes;
All was forgeten, and that was sene.
For al the woode was waxen grene;
Swetnesse of dew had mad hyt waxe.

The dreamer is now in a thick forest, with countless animals in it. Here he sees a man in black, sitting with his back against a thick oak. He tells the dreamer his tragic tale, describing in the following lines how Fortune played him at chess and turned 'all his wele to wo' (618ff).

For fals Fortune hath pleyd a game
Atte ches with me, allas the while!

404-9: trowe] *think*   envye wolde] *would aspire*   swiche seven] *seven times as many*   welken] *night sky*
410-15: morwes] *mornings*   his sorwes] *its pains*   sene] *evident*

The trayteresse fals and ful of gyle,   620
That al behoteth and nothing halt,
She goth upryght and yet she halt,
That baggeth foule and loketh faire,
The dispitouse debonaire
That skorneth many a creature!
An ydole of fals portrayture
Ys she, for she wil sone wrien;
She is the monstres heed ywrien,
As filth over-ystrawed with floures;
Hir moste worship and hir flour ys   630
To lyen, for that ys hyr nature;
Withoute feyth, lawe, or mesure.
She ys fals, and ever laughynge
With oon eye, and that other wepynge.
That ys broght up she set al doun.
I lykne hyr to the scorpioun,
That ys a fals, flaterynge beste;
For with his hede he maketh feste,
But al amydde hys flaterynge

620–9: behoteth] *promises*   halt] *holds to promise*   halt] *limps*   baggeth]
squints   dispitouse debonair] *scornful beauty*   wrien] *turn away*   ywrien]
covered   ystrawed] *strewn*
630–9: flour] *delight*   lawe] *rule*   mesure] *moderation*   That ys] *whatever
is*   maketh feste] *celebrates*

9

With hys tayle he wol stynge   640
And envenyme; and so wol she.
She is th'envyouse charite
That ys ay fals, and semeth wel;
So turneth she hyr false whel
Aboute, for hyt ys nothyng stable –
Now by the fire, now at table;
Ful many oon hath she thus yblent.
She ys pley of enchauntement,
That semeth oon and ys not soo.
The false thef! What hath she doo,   650
Trowest thou? By oure Lord, I wol the seye.
At the ches with me she gan to pleye;
With hir false draughtes dyvers
She staal on me, and tok my fers.
And whan I sawgh my fers awaye,
Allas, I kouthe no lenger playe,
But seyde 'Farewel, swete, ywys,
And farewel al that ever ther ys!'
Therwith Fortune seyde, 'Chek her!'

640–9: envenyme] *poison*   envyouse] *competitive*   ay] *always*   wel] *well
disposed*   yblent] *blinded*   pley] *pretence*   semeth oon] *seems one thing*
650–9: false draughtes dyvers] *many hostile moves*   staal] *stole up*   fers] *queen*
aweye] *gone*   Chek her] *Checkmate*

10

And 'Mat!' in the myd poynt of the chekker   660
With a poun erraunt, allas!
Ful craftier to pley she was
Than Athalus, that made the game
First of the ches: so was hys name.

The Man in Black describes his falling in love with his lady called 'goode faire White', whose name is taken to refer to Blanche of Lancaster, John of Gaunt's wife. The long love-description of her draws eloquently on the French Romance tradition. Only at the very end does the dreamer realise that the turning of 'wele to wo' for the Black Knight was her death. 'Is that youre los? By God, hyt ys routhe' (pity), he says. 'This kyng' rides homeward to his 'long castel' (Lancaster) on a 'ryche hil' (Richmond: Gaunt was Earl of Richmond as well as Lancaster). And the dreamer is woken by the castle bell in the dream (1321 ff).

Ryght thus me mette, as I yow telle,
That in the castell ther was a belle,
As hyt hadde smyten hours twelve.
Therwyth I awook myselve

660–4: chekker] *chessboard*   poun erraunt] *travelling pawn*
Athalus] *Attalus (III) Philometor Euergetes*
1321–4: me mette] *I dreamed*   smyten] *struck*

11

And fond me lyinge in my bed;
And the book that I had red,
Of Alcione and Seys the kyng,
And of the goddess of slepyng,
I fond hyt in myn hond ful even.
Thoghte I, 'Thys ys so queynt a sweven   1330
That I wol, be processe of tyme,
Fonde to put this sweven in ryme
As I kan best, and that anoon.'
This was my sweven; now hit ys doon.

꙳

1325–9: Alcione and Seys the kyng] *Alcyone and King Ceyx*   ful even] *simply*
1330–4: sweven] *dream*   Fonde] *attempt*   anoon] *soon*

The House of Fame

❦

Т*he House of Fame* is the most temptingly enigmatic of Chaucer's works. Written probably ten years after *The Book of the Duchess*, in about 1379, it has been described as the last substantial work of Chaucer's 'French period' before he became principally inspired by the works of his great Italian predecessors, Dante, Petrarch and Boccaccio. But it is an impressively classical and philosophically informed poem too. It begins where *The Book of the Duchess* ended, with a meditation on the authority of dreams, like the 'sweven' that ended the earlier poem. But this dreamer has a very different tone of voice from *The Book of the Duchess*'s uncertain narrator, who was slow on the uptake and whose primary concern was insomnia. This narrator ponders the causes of dreams as classically explained, wondering if it is sometimes 'the cruel life unsoft / Which these ilke lovers leden / That hopen over-muche or dreden' (36–8) – like the Man in Black. The narrator appeals again to the 'god of slep' in the following 'Invocation', but suddenly he gains his courage with a vengeance, in an opinionated outburst against those sceptical of the authority of dreams (like the sceptical rationalists who tend to be villains in Shakespeare – Edmund and Goneril and Regan in *King Lear*, for example). Having prayed at the very start that 'God turne us every drem to goode', the narrator prays that the god of sleep will cause him to prosper (77ff):

> And to this god, that I of rede
> Prey I that he wol me spede
> My sweven for to telle aryght,
> Yf every drem stonde in his myght.   80
> And he that mover ys of al
> That is and was and ever shal,
> So yive hem joye that hyt here
> Of alle that they dreme to-yere,
> And for to stonden alle in grace
> Of her loves, or in what place
> That hem were levest for to stonde,
> And shelde hem fro poverte and shonde
> And from unhap and ech disese,
> And sende hem al that may hem plese,   90
> That take hit wel and skorne hyt noght,

77–91: spede] *advance*   sweven] *dream*   might] *power*   to-yere] *this year*
levest] *most keen*   shonde] *shame*

Ne hyt mysdemen in her thought
Thorgh malicious entencion.
And whoso thorgh presumpcion,
Or hate, or skorn, or thorgh envye,
Dispit, or jape, or vilanye,
Mysdeme hyt, pray I Jesus God
That (dreme he barefot, dreme he shod),
That every harm that any man
Hath had syth the world began,   100
Befalle hym therof or he sterve,
And graunte he mote hit ful deserve,
Lo, with such a conclusion
As had of his avision
Cresus, that was kyng of Lyde,
That high upon a gebet dyde!
This prayer shal he have of me;
I am no bet in charyte!
Now herkeneth, as I have yow seyd,
What that I mette, or I abreyd.   110

92–110: mysdemen] *misinterpret*   whoso] *whoever*   Dispit] *spite*   jape] *joking*
shod] *wearing shoes*   syth] *since*   sterve] *dies*   mote] *may*   Lyde] *Lydia*
gebet] *gallows*   of me] *from me*   bet] *better*   mette] *dreamed*   or] *before*
abreyd] *woke up*

15

There follows the 'Story' of a dream that the narrator had on the tenth of December (we are given the date twice within fifty lines, though no particular significance is known for it). This, then, is another dream-poem; in its first book it sounds like a response to Virgil's *Aeneid*, telling the tragic story of Dido who hears of her abandonment by Aeneas from the many mouths and lips of *Fama*, Rumour, 'than whom no evil is swifter' (*Aeneid*, Book 4, 174). In Chaucer's Book 2, an eagle that the dreamer has seen at the end of Book 1 carries him high into the air, expounding the laws of physics as they go, to 'Geffrey', the dreamer. This bird, sent by Jupiter, praises Geffrey for his unrewarded literary service to love but mocks him for his bookishness:

> For when thy labour doon al ys,
> And hast mad alle thy rekenynges,
> In stede of reste and newe thynges
> Thou goost hom to thy hous anoon,
> And, also domb as any stoon,
> Thou sittest at another book
> Tyl fully daswed is thy look,
> And lyvest thus as an heremyte,
> Although thyn absstynence ys lyte.   660

652–60: also domb as] *as dumb as*   daswed] *dazed*

16

In recognition of his thankless service of Love, Jupiter's eagle carries him up towards the House of Fame (821) where they hear 'the grete soun . . . that rumbleth up and doun in fames house, ful of tydynges . . . of fals and soth compouned' (1029). On the way they see the great panorama of the upper air, notably the creatures that occupy the middle regions beween earth and sea and Heaven:

> Tho gan y loken under me
> And beheld the ayerissh bestes,
> Cloudes, mystes and tempestes,
> Snowes, hayles, reynes, wyndes,
> And th'engendrynge in hir kyndes
> All the wey thrugh which I cam.
> 'O God,' quod y, 'that made Adam,   970
> Moche ys thy might and thy noblesse!'
> And thoo thought y upon Boece,
> That writ, 'A thought may flee so hye
> Wyth fetheres of Philosophye,
> To passen everych element,
> And when he hath so fer ywent,

964–76: ayerissh] *aerial* bestes] *creatures* Boece] *Boethius*

> Than may be seen behynde hys bak
> Cloude' – and al that y of spak.

In Book 3, after the departure of the eagle, the dreamer examines this place, a mountain made of ice where the inscribed names melt away in the heat of the sun but stay legible where they face the cold north. He witnesses the appeals made to the whimsical Lady Fame who arbitrarily assigns celebrity or obscurity, and good or ill fame. Having declared his dismay at Fame's whimsy, he is led to a labyrinth, the House of Rumour, a spinning cage made of twigs. Confusion and interpretation become ever more impossible, even when the dreamer rediscovers his eagle (1990) who lifts him into the spinning wicker House of Rumour 'in his toes'. To understand the nature of this House, and its difference from the world of Fame or Fortuna, the best modern term is 'Gossip', where messages are exchanged by a kind of 'Chinese Whispers' (2060–75).

> Thus north and southe
> Went every word fro mouth to mouthe,
> And that encresing ever-mo,
> As fyr is wont to quikke and go

2075–8: quikke] *catch life*

From a sparke spronge amis,
Til al a citee brent up is.   2080
And whan that was ful yspronge,
And woxen more on every tonge
Than ever hit was, hit wente anoon
Up to a windowe, out to goon;
Or, but hit mighte out ther pace,
Hit gan out crepe at som crevace,
And fleigh forth faste for the nones.
And somtyme saugh I tho, at ones,
A lesing and a sad soth-sawe,
That gonne of aventure drawe   2090
Out at a windowe for to pace;
And, when they metten in that place,
They were achekked bothe two,
And neither of hem moste out go;
For other so they gonne croude,
Til eche of hem gan cryen loude,
'Lat me go first!' – 'Nay, but let me!
And here I wol ensuren thee

2079–90: spronge amis] *sparked out astray*   brent] *burnt*   that was ful
y-spronge] *that (story) had fully developed*   woxen] *grown*   out to goon] *to
escape*   but hit mighte] *if it couldn't*   crevace] *gap*   fleigh forth] *flew away*
for the nones] *then*   tho] *then*   lesing and a sad soth-sawe] *lie and a serious
truth*   of aventure] *by chance*
2091–8: achekked] *stopped*   moste] *could*   ensuren] *promise*

19

With the nones that thou wolt do so,
That I shal never fro thee go,   2100
But be thyn owne sworen brother!
We wil medle us ech with other,
That no man, be he never so wrothe,
Shal han that oon of two, but bothe
At ones, al beside his leve,
Come we a-morwe or on eve,
Be we cryed or stille yrouned.'
Thus saugh I fals and sooth compouned
Togeder flee for oo tydinge.
  Thus out at holes gonne wringe   2110
Every tyding streight to Fame;
And she gan yeven eche his name,
After hir disposicioun,
And yaf hem ek duracioun,
Some to wexe and wane sone,
As dooth the faire, whyte mone,
And leet hem gon. Ther might I seen
Wenged wondres faste fleen,

2099–110: With the nones that] *on the condition that*   medle] *mix*   wrothe] *at odds*   al beside his leve] *entirely against his will*   cryed or stille yrouned] *shouted out or whispered*   compouned] *mixed*   flee] *fly*   for oo tydinge] *as the same story*   wringe] *squeeze*
2111–18: yeven] *give*   disposicioun] *whim*   Wenged wondres] *marvels on wings*

Twenty thousand in a route,
As Eolus hem blew aboute.   2120
   And, lord! this hous, in alle tymes,
Was ful of shipmen and pilgrymes,
With scrippes bret-ful of lesinges,
Entremedled with tydinges,
And ek alone by hem-selve.
O, many a thousand tymes twelve
Saugh I ek of these pardoneres,
Currours, and ek messageres,
With boystes crammed ful of lyes
As ever vessel was with lyes.   2130
And as I alther-fastest wente
Aboute, and dide al myn entente
Me for to pleye and for to lere,
And ek a tyding for to here,
That I had herd of som contree
That shal not now be told for me; –
For hit no nede is, redely;
Folk can singe hit bet than I;

2119–30: route] *crowd*   scrippes] *bags*   bret-ful of lesinges] *brim-full of lies*
entremedled] *mixed*   tydinges] *messages*   Currours] *couriers*   boystes
containers   lyes] *dregs (lees)*
2131–8: alther-fastest] *fastest of all*   entente] *purpose*   ek] *every*   for me] *by me*
redely] *really*

21

For al mot out, other late or rathe,
Alle the sheves in the lathe; –   2140
I herde a gret noise withalle
In a corner of the halle,
Ther men of love tydings tolde,
And I gan thiderward beholde;
For I saugh renninge every wight,
As faste as that they hadden might;
And everich cryed, 'What thing is that?'
And som seyde, 'I not never what,'
And whan they were alle on an hepe,
Tho behinde gonne up lepe,   2150
And clamben up on othere faste,
And up the nose and yen caste,
And troden faste on othere heles,
And stampe, as men don after eles.
   Atte laste I saugh a man,
Which that I nevene naught ne can;
But he semed for to be
A man of greet auctoritee . . .

2139–58: mot] *must*   rathe] *early*   lathe] *barn*   as that they hadden might] *as
they could*   yen] *eyes*   after eles] *hunting eels*   nevene] *name*

These closing lines describe the excited, Dantesque stampede that arises in 'a corner of the halle / Ther men of love-tydynges tolde' where a figure of importance is rumoured to be appearing. But with the appearance of this 'man of greet auctoritee' the poem, frustratingly, ends. We can't know whether this was an abandoned project or an extreme example of a Chaucerian inconclusive ending, as in *The Parliament of Fowls* or *The Nun's Priest's Tale*, or, for that matter, *The Canterbury Tales* as a whole.

The Parliament of Fowls

‿

This poem, probably written in the early 1380s, before *Troilus and Criseyde* but later than the other dream-visions, was highly praised by C. S. Lewis in *The Allegory of Love* where he says 'every reader who loves poetry may safely be left alone with' this poem, 'like Mozartian music'. The poem certainly displays a classical elegance in the service of its traditional theme, despite the disparateness of its two halves. It starts with a classic application to Love of the Greek and Latin epigram about art: *ars longa, vita brevis*. The familiar Chaucerian narrator speaks of his bookishness and tells how reading Cicero's *Dream of Scipio* (in which the elder Scipio, Africanus, addresses his grandson, Aemilianus, in a dream) causes the poem's narrator to have the St Valentine's Day dream about the bird-debate that takes up the second half of the poem and gives it its title.

The lyf so short, the craft so long to lerne,
Th'assay so hard, so sharp the conquerynge,
The dredful joye alwey that slit so yerne:
Al this mene I by Love, that my felynge
Astonyeth with his wonderful werkynge
So sore, iwis, that whan I on hym thynke
Nat wot I wel wher that I flete or synke.   7

For al be that I knowe nat Love in dede,
Ne wot how that he quiteth folk here hyre,
Yet happeth me ful ofte in bokes rede
Of his myrakles, and his crewel yre.
There rede I wel he wol be lord and syre;
I dar nat seyn, his strokes been so sore,
But 'God save swich a lord!' – I can na moore.   14

Of usage – what for lust and what for lore –
On bokes rede I ofte, as I yow tolde.
But wherfore that I speke al this? Nat yoore
Agon it happede me for to beholde

1–7: craft] *skill*   assay] *attempt*   slit so yerne] *slips away so fast*   mene] *refer to*
Astonyeth] *is dazed*   flete or synke] *sink or swim*
8–14: in dede] *in practice*   quiteth] *repays*   hyre] *toil*   syre] *master*   dar nat
seyn . . . But] *can only say*
15–18: what for lust] *whether for desire*   yoore] *long ago*   beholde] *look at*

Upon a boke, was write with lettres olde,
And therupon, a certeyn thing to lerne,
The longe day ful faste I redde and yerne.　　　　21

For out of olde feldes, as men seyth,
Cometh al this newe corn fro yer to yere,
And out of olde bokes, in good feyth,
Cometh al this newe science that men lere.
But now to purpos as of this matere:
To rede forth hit gan me so delite,
That al that day me thoughte but a lyte.　　　　28

This bok of which I make mencioun
Entitled was al ther, as I shal telle:
'Tullyus of the Drem of Scipioun.'
Chapitres sevene it hadde, of hevene and helle
And erthe, and soules that therinne dwelle,
Of whiche, as shortly as I can it trete,
Of his sentence I wol you seyn the greete.　　　　35

19–21: redde] *read*　yerne] *eagerly*
22–8: men seyth] *they say*　science] *knowledge*　lere] *learn*　to purpos] *to the point*　a lyte] *a short time*
29–35: Tullyus] *Cicero*　sentence] *meaning*　greete] *most part*

The book describes the exchanges between Scipio and the Numidian king Masinissa, and the poet reads until it becomes too dark to read any longer (85ff).

> The day gan faylen, and the derke nyght,
> That reveth bestes from here besynesse,
> Berafte me my bok for lak of lyght,
> And to my bed I gan me for to dresse,
> Fulfyld of thought and besy hevynesse;
> For bothe I hadde thyng which that I nolde,
> And ek I ne hadde that thyng that I wolde.   91

> But fynally my spirit at the laste,
> For wery of my labour al the day,
> Tok reste, that made me to slepe faste;
> And in my slep I mette, as that I lay,
> How Affrican, ryght in the selve aray
> That Scipion hym say byfore that tyde,
> Was come and stod right at my beddes syde.   98

85–91: Berafte] *deprived*   dresse] *approach*   besy] *anxious*   ek] *also*
92–8: For wery] *through weariness*   faste] *deeply*   mette] *dreamed*
Affrican] *Scipio the Elder*

28

The wery huntere, slepynge in his bed,
To wode ayeyn his mynde goth anon;
The juge dremeth how his plees ben sped;
The cartere dremeth how his cart is gon;
The riche, of gold; the knyght fight with his fon;
The syke met he drynketh of the tonne;
The lovere met he hath his lady wonne.   105

By the same tendency of waking thoughts to prompt the substance
of the dream, the narrator dreams that Scipio (Affrican) leads him
into a garden with Dantesque inscriptions over the gates and guides
him as Virgil guided Dante (120ff).

This forseyde Affrican me hente anon
And forth with hym unto a gate brought,
Ryght of a park walled with grene ston;
And over the gate, with lettres large iwroughte,
There were vers iwriten, as me thoughte,
On eyther half, of ful gret difference,
Of which I shal yow seyn the pleyn sentence: 126

99–105: To wode] *to the woods*   ben sped] *have fared*   fon] *enemies*   syke] *sick
person*   tonne] *cask*   met] *dreams*
120–6: hente] *seized hold*   iwroughte] *written*   sentence] *meaning*

'Thorgh me men gon into that blysful place
Of hertes hele and dedly woundes cure;
Thorgh me men gon unto the welle of grace,
There grene and lusty May shal evere endure;
This is the wey to al good aventure.
Be glad, thow redere, and thy sorwe of-caste,
Al open am I – passe in, and sped thee faste!'   133

'Thorgh me men gon,' than spak that other syde,
'Unto the mortal strokes of the spere
Of which Disdayn and Daunger is the gyde,
Ther nevere tre shal fruyt ne leves bere.
This strem yow ledeth to the sorweful were
There as the fish in prysoun is al drye;
Th'eschewing is only the remedye.'   140

These vers of gold and blak iwriten were,
Of whiche I gan astoned to beholde,
For with that oon encresed ay my fere
And with that other gan myn herte bolde;

127–33: hele] *health*   There] *where*   aventure] *experience*   sped thee faste]
succeed fully
134–40: Daunger] *Discouragement*   Ther] *where*   were] *weir*   eschewing]
avoidance
141–4: astoned] *bewildered*

That oon me hette, that other dide me colde,
No wit hadde I, for errour, for to chese
To entre or flen, or me to save or lese.   147

Right as betwixen adamauntes two
Of evene myght, a pece of yren set
Ne hath no myght to meve to ne fro –
For what that oon may hale, that other let –
Ferde I, that nyste whether me was bet
To entre or leve, til Affrycan, my gide,
Me hente and shof in at the gates wide,   154

And seyde, 'It stondeth writen in thy face,
Thyn errour, though thow telle it not to me;
But dred the not to come into this place,
For this writyng nys nothyng ment bi the,
Ne by non but he Loves servaunt be:
For thow of love hast lost thy tast, I gesse,
As sek man hath of swete and bytternesse.   161

145–7: chese] *choose*   flen] *flee*
148–54: adamauntes magnets evene] *equal*   hale] *attract*   let] *repel*
shof] *shoved*
155–61: nys nothyng ment] *does not apply*   sek] *sick*

31

'But natheles, although that thow be dul,
Yit that thow canst not do, yit mayst thou se.
For many a man that may not stonde a pul
Yet liketh hym at wrastlyng for to be,
And demen yit wher he do bet or he.
And if thow haddest connyng for t'endite,
I shal the shewe mater of to wryte.'   168

With that myn hand in his he took anon,
Of which I confort caughte, and wente in faste.
But, Lord! so I was glad and wel begoon!
For overal where that I myne eyen caste
Were trees clad with leves that ay shal laste,
Ech in his kynde, of colour fresh and greene
As emeraude, that joye was to seene.   175

The byldere ok, and ek the hardy asshe;
The piler elm, the cofre unto careyne;
The boxtre pipere, holm to whippes lashe;
The saylynge firr; the cipresse, deth to pleyne;

162–8: stonde a pul] *offer a contest*   he do bet or he] *one person or another does better*   connyng] *skill*
169–75: wel begoon] *happily placed*   overal where] *wherever*   ay] *for ever*
in his kynde] *by its nature*
176–9: byldere] *for building*   piler] *pillar*   cofre unto careyne] *coffin for corpses*   pipere] *for pipes*   holm] *holly*   pleyne] *lament*

The shetere ew, the asp for shaftes pleyne;
The olyve of pes, and eke the dronke vyne;
The victor palm, the laurer to devyne.   182

A gardyn saw I ful of blosmy bowes,
Upon a ryver, in a grene mede,
There as swetnesse everemore inow is,
With floures white, blewe, yelwe, and rede,
And colde welle-stremes, nothyng dede,
That swymmen ful of smale fishes lighte,
With fynnes rede and skales sylver bryghte.   189

On every bow the bryddes herde I synge,
With voys of aungel in here armonye;
Som besyede hem here bryddes forth to brynge;
The litel conyes to here pley gonne hye.
And ferther al aboute I gan espye
The dredful ro, the buk, the hert and hynde,
Squyrels, and bestes smale of gentil kinde.   196

180–2: shetere] *shooter*   asp] *aspen*   dronke] *drunken*   laurer to devyne]
divining laurel
183–9: inow] *much*   nothyng] *anything but*
190–6: here] *their*   bryddes] *nestlings*   conyes] *rabbits*   hye] *hasten*
dredful] *timid*   gentil] *noble*

Of instruments of strenges in acord
Herde I so pleye a ravyshyng swetnesse,
That God, that makere is of al and lord,
Ne herde nevere beter, as I gesse.
Therwith a wynd, unnethe it myghte be lesse,
Made in the leves grene a noyse softe
Acordaunt to the foules songe alofte. 203

Th'air of that place so attempre was
That nevere was grevaunce of hot ne cold.
There wex ek every holsom spice and gras;
No man may there waxe sek ne old;
Yit was there joye more a thousandfold
Than man can telle; ne nevere wolde it nyghte,
But ay cler day to any mannes syghte. 210

Under a tre, besyde a welle, I say
Cupide, oure lord, his arwes forge and file,
And at his fet his bowe al redy lay;
And Wille, his doughter, temprede al this while

197–203: acord] *unison*   unnethe] *hardly*   Acordaunt] *attuned to*
204–10: attempre] *temperate*   grevaunce] *discomfort*   nyghte] *become*
night   ay] *always*
211–14: say] *saw*

The hevedes in the welle, and with hire wile
She couchede hem, after they shulde serve:
Some for to sle, and some to wounde and kerve.   217

Tho was I war of Plesaunce anon-ryght,
And of Aray, and Lust, and Curteysie,
And of the Craft that can and hath the myght
To don by force a wight to don folye –
Disfigurat was she, I nyl not lye;
And by hymself, under an oke, I gesse,
Saw I Delyt, that stod with Gentilesse.   224

Scipio disappears from the scene without explanation, and the dreamer sees the various allegorical figures of the love-garden, culminating in a vision of the goddess Nature, before whom the birds come to choose their mates (308ff).

For this was on Seynt Valentynes day,
Whan every foul cometh there to chese his make,
Of every kynde that men thynke may,

215–17: hevedes] *arrowheads*   wile] *skill*   couchede] *placed*
218–24: Tho] *then*   anon-ryght] *right away*   Aray] *clothing*   Lust] *desire*
don] *make*   wight] *person*   Gentilesse] *Nobility*

And that so huge a noyse gan they make,
That erthe, and eyr, and tre, and every lake
So ful was that unethe was there space
For me to stonde, so ful was al the place.   315

And right as Aleyn, in the Pleynt of Kinde,
Devyseth Nature of aray and face,
In swich aray men myghte hire there fynde.
This noble emperesse, ful of grace,
Bad every foul to take his owne place,
As they were woned alwey fro yer to yeere,
Seynt Valentynes day, to stonden there.   322

That is to seyn, the foules of ravine
Weere hyest set, and thanne the foules smale
That eten, as hem nature wolde enclyne,
As worm or thyng of which I telle no tale;
And water-foul sat lowest in the dale;
But foul that lyveth by sed sat on the grene,
And that so fele that wonder was to sene.   329

312–15: make] *mate*
316–22: Aleyn] *Alain de l'Isle, twelfth-century author of* De Planctu Naturae (the
Pleynt of Kynde)   Devyseth] *describes*   aray] *dress*   woned] *wont*
323–9: foules of ravine] *birds of prey*   eten] *eat*   As] *such things as*   dale]
valley   sed] *seed*   fele] *numerous*

There myghte men the royal egle fynde,
That with his sharpe lok perseth the sonne,
And other egles of a lowere kinde,
Of whiche that clerkes wel devyse conne.
Ther was the tiraunt with his fetheres donne
And grey – I mene the goshauk that doth pyne
To bryddes for his outrageous ravyne.   336

The gentyl faucoun, that with his feet distrayneth
The kynges hand; the hardy sperhauk eke,
The quayles foo; the merlioun that payneth
Himself ful ofte the larke for to seke;
Ther was the douve with hire yen meke;
The jelous swan, ayens his deth that syngeth;
The oule ek, that of deth the bode bringeth;   343

The crane, the geaunt, with his trompes soun;
The thef, the chough; and ek the janglynge pye;
The skornynge jay; the eles fo, heroun;
The false lapwynge, ful of trecherye;

330-6: perseth] *looks at*   devyse] *describe*   donne] *brown*   pyne] *suffering*
337-43: gentyl] *noble*   distrayneth] *grasps*   sperhauk] *sparrowhawk*   yen] *eyes*
bode] *foreboding*
344-7: geaunt] *giant*   trompes] *trumpet*   ek] *also*   pye] *magpie*

The stare, that the conseyl can bewrye;
The tame ruddok, and the coward kyte;
The cok, that orloge is of thorpes lyte;   350

The sparow, Venus sone; the nyghtyngale
That clepeth forth the grene leves newe;
The swalwe, mortherere of the foules smale
That maken hony of floures freshe of hewe;
The wedded turtil, with hire herte trewe;
The pekok, with his aungels fetheres bryghte;
The fesaunt, skornere of the cok by nyghte;   357

The waker goos; the cukkow ever unkinde;
The popynjay, ful of delicasye;
The drake, stroyere of his owene kynde;
The stork, the wrekere of avouterye;
The hote cormeraunt of glotenye;
The raven wys, the crowe with vois of care;
The throstil olde; the frosty feldefare.   364

348–50: stare] *starling*   bewrye] *betray*   ruddok] *robin*   orloge] *clock*
thorpes lyte] *small villages*
351–7: foules] *bees*   turtil] *turtle-dove*
358–64: waker] *watchful*   popynjay] *parrot*   delicasye] *wantonness*   stroyere]
destroyer   wrekere] *punisher*   avouterye] *adultery*   frosty] *in the frosty season*

38

Nature, who has a beautiful female eagle on her wrist, declares that all the bird species must choose their mates, beginning with the eagle, the bird of highest degree. A noble 'tercel', a male eagle, speaks first, of his love for the female on Nature's wrist. But a second noble male declares that he has loved this female longer, and a third that he has loved her more deeply. The dreamer is impressed by the elegance of their speeches, but the other birds, who want to get on with their choosing, are less impressed (484ff).

> Of al my lyf, syn that day I was born,
> So gentil ple in love or other thyng
> Ne herde nevere no man me beforn –
> Who that hadde leyser and connyng
> For to reherse hire chere and hire spekyng;
> And from the morwe gan this speche laste
> Tyl dounward went the sonne wonder faste.   490
>
> The noyse of foules for to ben delyvered
> So loude rong, 'Have don, and lat us wende!'
> That wel wende I the wode hadde al to-shyvered.

484–90: Of al my lyf] *in all my life*   So gentil ple] *such noble pleading*   Who that hadde] *if anyone had*   chere] *demeanour*
491–3: noyse] *clamour*   delyvered] *released*   Have don] *finish up*   wende] *go*   wende] *thought*   to-shyvered] *shattered*

'Com of!' they criede, 'allas, ye wol us shende!
Whan shal your cursede pletynge have an ende?
How sholde a juge eyther parti leve
For ye or nay withouten any preve?'   497

The goos, the cokkow, and the doke also
So cryede, 'Kek, kek! kokkow! quek, quek!' hye,
That thourgh myne eres the noyse wente tho.
The goos seyde, 'Al this nys not worth a flye!
But I can shape herof a remedie,
And I wol seye my verdit fayre and swythe
For water-foul, whoso be wroth or blythe.'   504

'And I for worm-foul,' seyde the fol kokkow,
'For I wol of myn owene autorite,
For comune spede, take on the charge now,
For to delyvere us is gret charite.'
'Ye may abyde a while yit, parde!'
Quod the turtel, 'if it be youre wille
A wight may speke, hym were as good be stille.   511

494-7: Com of!] *Come on!*   shende] *ruin*   pletynge] *debating*   leve] *believe*
preve] *proof*
498-504: tho] *then*   swythe] *firmly*   For] *on behalf of*   wroth] *angry*
505-11: worm-foul] *worm-eating birds*   comune spede] *general good*   charge]
issue   delyvere] *release*   hym were as good] *he might as well*

'I am a sed-foul, oon the unworthieste,
That wot I wel, and litel of connynge.
But bet is that a wyghtes tonge reste
Than entermeten hym of such doinge
Of which he neyther rede can ne synge;
And whoso hit doth ful foule hymself acloyeth,
For office uncommytted ofte anoyeth.'   518

Nature, which that alwey hadde an ere
To murmur of the lewednesse behynde,
With facound voys seyde, 'Hold youre tonges there!
And I shal sone, I hope, a conseyl fynde
Yow to delyvere, and fro this noyse unbynde;
I juge, of every folk men shul oon calle
To seyn the verdit for yow foules alle.'   525

Assented were to this conclusioun
The briddes alle; and foules of ravine
Han chosen fyrst, by pleyn eleccioun,
The tercelet of the faucoun to diffyne

512–18: sed-foul] *seed-eater*   connynge] *understanding*   wyghtes] *creature's*
entermeten] *interfere*   rede] *advise*   acloyeth] *overburdens*   office] *service*
uncommytted] *uninvited*
519–25: hadde an ere] *listened out for*   murmur] *grumbling*   lewednesse
behynde] *ignorant classes*   facound] *eloquent*   conseyl] *judge*   noyse]
clamour   unbynde] *set free*   I juge] *I declare*   verdit] *verdict*
526–9: foules of ravine] *birds of prey*   pleyn eleccioun] *simple choice*   tercelet of
the faucoun] *male falcon*   diffyne] *declare*

Al here sentence, and as him list, termyne;
And to Nature hym gonne to presente,
And she accepteth hym with glad entente.   532

The terslet seyde thanne in this manere:
'Ful hard were it to preve by resoun
Who loveth best this gentil formel heere;
For everych hath swich replicacioun
That non by skilles may be broght adoun;
I can not se that argumentes avayle;
Thanne semeth it there moste be batayle.'   539

'Al redy!' quod these egles tercels tho.
'Nay, sires' quod he, 'if that I durste it seye,
Ye don me wrong, my tale is not ido!
For, sires – ne taketh not agref I preye –
It may not gon, as ye wolde in this weye;
Oure is the voys that han the charge in honde,
And to the juges dom ye moten stonde.   546

530–2: list] *chose*   termyne] *give a final verdict*
533–9: formel] *female*   replicacioun] *answer*   skilles] *arguments*   broght
adoun] *refuted*
540–6: tercels] *males*   durste] *dared*   ido] *finished*   agref] *amiss*   gon]
succeed   charge] *commission*   dom] *judgement*   stonde] *abide by*

'And therfore pes! I seye, as to my wit,
Me wolde thynke how that the worthieste
Of knyghthod, and lengest had used hit,
Most of estat, of blod the gentilleste,
Were sittingest for hire, if that hir leste;
And of these thre she wot hireself, I trowe,
Which that he be, for it is light to knowe.'   553

The water-foules han here hedes leid
Togedere, and of a short avysement,
Whan everych hadde his large golee seyd,
They seyden sothly, al by oon assent,
How that the goos, with here facounde gent,
'That so desyreth to pronounce oure nede,
Shal telle our tale,' and preyede 'God hire spede.'   560

And for these water-foules tho began
The goos to speke, and in hire kakelynge
She seyde, 'Pes! Now tak kep every man,
And herkeneth which a resoun I shal forth bringe;

547–53: lengest] *for the longest time*   estat] *social status*   gentilleste] *noblest*
sittingest] *most suitable*   light] *easy*
554–60: leid / Togedere] *put together*   avysement] *deliberation*   large golee]
throatful   facounde gent] *noble eloquence*
561–4: tho] *then*   tak kep] *take note*   resoun] *argument*

My wit is sharp; I love no taryinge:
I seye I rede hym, though he were my brother,
But she wol love hym, lat him love another!'   567

'Lo, here a parfit reson of a goos!'
Quod the sperhauk; 'Nevere mot she thee!
Lo, swich it is to have a tonge loos!
Now parde, fol, yit were it bet for the
Han holde thy pes than shewed thy nycete.
It lyth not in his wit, ne in his wille,
But soth is seyd, "a fol can not be stille." '   574

The laughter aros of gentil foules alle,
And right anon the sed-foul chosen hadde
The turtle trewe, and gonne hire to hem calle,
And preyeden hire to seyn the sothe sadde
Of this matere, and axede what she radde;
And she answerde that pleynly hire entente
She wolde shewe, and sothly what she mente.   581

568–74: thee] *prosper*   nycete] *stupidity*   It lyth not] *it isn't*   soth] *truth*
575–81: sadde] *reliable*   radde] *advised*   entente] *opinion*

'Nay, God forbede a lovere shulde chaunge!'
The turtle seyde, and wex for shame al red;
'Though that his lady everemore be straunge,
Yit lat hym serve hire ever, til he be ded;
Forsothe, I preyse nat the goses red;
For thogh she deyede, I wolde non other make,
I wol ben hires, til that the deth me take.'   588

'Wel bourded' quod the doke, 'by myn hat!
That men shulde loven alwey causeless!
Who can a reson fynde or wit in that?
Daunceth he murye that is myrtheles?
Who shulde recche of that is recheles?'
'Ye queke,' seyde the goos, 'ful wel and fayre!
There been mo sterres, God wot, than a payre!'   595

'Now fy, cherl!' quod the gentil tercelet,
'Out of the donghil com that word ful right,
Thou canst noght see which thing is wel beset:
Thou farest by love as oules doon by light,

582–8: wex] *became*   straunge] *remote*   red] *advice*   make] *mate*
589–95: Wel bourded] *Well joked!*   recche of that] *care about what*   recheles]
unregarding   Ye queke] *you're speaking*   God wot] *God knows*
596–9: fy] *shame*   cherl] *peasant*   donghil] *dung-heap*   wel beset] *properly
judged*

45

The day hem blent, ful wel they see by night;
Thy kind is of so lowe a wrechednesse,
That what love is, thou canst nat see ne gesse.'   602

Tho gan the kokkow putte hym forth in pres
For foul that eteth worm, and seyde blyve,
'So I,' quod he, 'may have my make in pes,
I reche nat how longe that ye stryve;
Lat ech of hem be soleyn al here lyve!
This is my reed, sin they may not acorde;
This shorte lessoun nedeth nat recorde.'   609

'Ye, have the glotoun fild inow his paunche,
Thanne are we wel!' seyde the merlioun;
'Thou mortherere of the heysoge on the braunche
That broughte the forth, thou reufullest glotoun!
Lyve thow soleyn, wormes corupcioun!
For no fors is of lak of thy nature!
Go, lewed be thow whil the world may dure!'   616

600–2: blent] *blinds*
603–9: in pres] *into the fight*   For] *on behalf of*   blyve] *quickly*   So] *so long as*
stryve] *argue*   soleyn] *single*   recorde] *be repeated on and on*
610–16: paunche] *stomach*   heysoge] *hedge sparrow*   reufullest] *wretched*
no fors is] *it doesn't matter*   thy nature] *the likes of you*   lewed be thou] *stay*
ignorant   dure] *last*

46

'Now pes,' quod Nature, 'I comaunde here;
For I have herd al your opynyoun,
And in effect yit be we nevere the neer.
But fynally, this is my conclusioun,
That she hireself shal han hir eleccioun
Of whom hire lest, whoso be wroth or blythe,
Hym that she cheest, he shal hire han as swithe.   623

'For sith it may not here discussed be
Who loveth hire best, as seyde the tercelet,
Thanne wol I don hire this favour, that she
Shal han right hym on whom hire herte is set,
And he hire that his herte hath on hir knet.
Thus Iuge I, Nature, for I may not lye;
To non estat I have non other ye.   630

'But as for counseyl for to chese a make,
If hit were Resoun, certes thanne wolde I
Conseyle yow the royal tercel take,
As seyde the tercelet ful skylfully,

617–23: the neer] *nearer a conclusion*   hire lest] *she wants*   as swithe]
immediately
624–30: sith] *since*   on hire knet] *joined to her*   estat] *social status*   non other
ye] *any other view*
631–4: counseyl] *advice*   Resoun] *rational*   skylfully] *rationally*

As for the gentilleste and most worthi,
Which I have wrought so wel to my plesaunce
That to yow hit oughte to been a suffisaunce.'   637

With dredful vois the formel hire answerde,
'My rightful lady, goddesse of Nature,
Soth is that I am evere under youre yerde,
As is everich other creature,
And mot be youres whil my lyf may dure;
And therfore graunteth me my firste bone,
And myn entente I wol yow sey right sone.'   644

'I graunte it yow,' quod she; and right anon
This formel egle spak in this degree:
'Almyghty quene, unto this yer be don
I axe respit for to avise me.
And after that to have my choys al fre;
This al and som that I wol speke and seye;
Ye gete no more, although ye do me deye.   651

635-7: As for] *as*   to my plesaunce] *according to my wish*
638-44: dredful] *fearful*   formel] *female*   yerde] *control*   bone] *favour*
645-51: in this degree] *to this effect*   unto] *until*   don] *over*   avise] *consider*

48

'I wol noght serven Venus ne Cupide
Forsothe as yit, by no manere weye.'
'Now, syn it may non otherwise betyde,'
Quod Nature, 'heere is no more to seye;
Thanne wolde I that these foules were aweye,
Ech with his make, for taryinge lengere heere' –
And seyde hem thus, as ye shul after here.   658

'To you speke I, ye tercelets,' quod Nature,
'Beth of good herte and serveth, alle three.
 A yer is nat so longe to endure,
And ech of yow peyne him in his degre
For to do wel, for, God wot, quyt is she
Fro yow this yeer; what after so befalle,
This entremes is dressed for you alle.'   665

And whan this werk al brought was to an ende,
To every foul Nature yaf his make
By evene acord, and on here way they wende.
And, Lord, the blisse and joye that they make!

652–8: Forsothe] *certainly*   aweye] *on their way*   for taryinge] *to avoid delaying*
659–65: serveth] *do noble service*   peyne] *take pains*   in his degre] *according to his status*   what] *whatever*   entremes is dressed] *between-courses dish is prepared*
666–9: yaf] *gave*   evene acord] *general agreement*

49

For ech of hem gan other in wynges take,
And with here nekkes ech gan other wynde,
Thankynge alwey the noble goddesse of kinde.　　　672

But fyrst were chosen foules for to synge,
As yer by yer was alwey hir usaunce
To synge a roundel at here departynge,
To don Nature honour and plesaunce.
The note, I trowe, imaked was in Fraunce;
The wordes were swiche as ye may heer fynde,
The nexte vers, as I now have in mynde.　　　679

'Now welcome, somer, with thy sonne softe,
That hast thes wintres wedres overshake,
And driven away the longe nyghtes blake!

'Saynt Valentyn, that art ful hy on-lofte,
Thus syngen smale foules for thy sake:
　(Now welcome, somer, with thy sonne softe,
　That hast thes wintres weders overshake.)　　　686

670–2: wynde] *embrace*　alwey] *incessantly*
673–9: usaunce] *practice*　roundel] *refrain song*　trowe] *imagine*
680–6: wedres] *storms*　overshake] *shaken off*　on-lofte] *on high*

'Wel han they cause for to gladen ofte,
Sith ech of hem recovered hath hys make;
Ful blisful may they singen whan they wake:
  (Now welcome somer, with thy sonne softe,
  That hast thes wintres weders overshake,
  And driven away the longe nyghtes blake.')   692

And with the shoutyng, whan the song was do
That foules maden at hir flight a-way,
I wook, and othere bokes took me to
To reede upon, and yit I rede alwey;
I hope, ywis, to rede so som day
That I shal mete som thyng for to fare
The bet; and thus to rede I nyl nat spare.   699

&

687–92: gladen] *rejoice*   Sith] *since*
693–9: do / That foules maden] *caused the birds* to   yit] *still*   mete]
dream   fare] *prosper*   bet] *better*   spare] *neglect*

Troilus and Criseyde

᎗

E ven though Chaucer's most monumental and celebrated achieve-
ment is *The Canterbury Tales*, on which he was working to
the very end of his life, none of the tales, or no part of them, can
compare as a single poem with his great tragic romance *Troilus
and Criseyde*, written when the poet was at the height of his powers
between 1385 and 1388. Without it there would be nothing to show
that Chaucer had the Coleridgean 'shaping power of imagination' to
complete a large sustained canvas. If any of Chaucer's writings can
rebut Arnold's accusation that he lacked 'high seriousness', it is this.
Troilus is a loose translation of Boccaccio's lyrical and sentimental
love-elegy *Il Filostrato*, but it entirely transcends its model, bringing
to the story a philosophical range, practicality and humanity
which establish it as the first great long poem in English, ranking
with *Paradise Lost* and *The Prelude*. It outclasses in humane serious-
ness the Shakespeare plays which are indebted to it, *Troilus and
Cressida* and *Romeo and Juliet*. It is more reminiscent of *Antony
and Cleopatra* in its mixture of passion and folly and humanity and
calculation.

From its opening lines the poem's outcome is never in doubt. We are told that Troilus' 'double sorrow' will take him from misery to happiness, 'and after out of joy' when Criseyde abandons him for Diomede. But Chaucer uses the tyranny of the received story to create a sense of the tragic inescapability of life: Criseyde knows she is fated to have for ever the name of love traitress (in the second-last extract here), but what can she do, 'with women fewe, among the Grekis stronge'? In the first three of the poem's five books Troilus and his crony Pandarus (Criseyde's uncle) bring about the passionate love affair that lasts for three years, before Criseyde leaves to join her father Calchas in the Greek camp, exchanged for the real traitor Antenor. Heartbroken at the loss of her, Troilus throws himself with abandon into the fighting before Troy, until his inevitable death at the hands of Achilles: 'despitously him slewe the fierce Achille'.

It is the compelling character of Criseyde that sustains mystery in the development of this story which gives the outcome away from the start. This is evident in her first appearance, when it is puzzlingly difficult to tell whether she is defiantly confident or already what the poem later calls 'the ferfulleste wight that mighte ben' (Book 2, 450–1): the most frightened person possible. Troilus first sees her in the Chaucerian season of April as they all do observance in the Temple:

And so bifel, whan comen was the tyme   155
Of Aperil, whan clothed is the mede
With newe grene, of lusty Veer the pryme,
And swote smellen floures white and rede,
In sondry wises shewed, as I rede,
The folk of Troie hire observaunces olde,   160
Palladiones feste for to holde.

And to the temple, in al hir beste wise,
In general ther wente many a wight,
To herknen of Palladions servyse;
And namely, so many a lusty knyght,   165
So many a lady fressh and mayden bright,
Ful wel arayed, both meeste, mene, and leste,
Ye, bothe for the seson and the feste.

Among thise othere folk was Criseyda,
In widewes habit blak; but natheles,   170
Right as our firste lettre is now an A,
In beaute first so stood she, makeles;

155–61: the mede] *the meadow*   of lusty Veer the pryme] *the start of delightful spring*   swote] *sweet*   shewed . . . hire observaunces] *made their devotions*   Palladiones feste] *the feast of Pallas Athene*
162–8: to herknen of Palladions servyse] *to listen to the service of Pallas*   namely] *that is to say*   meeste, mene, and leste] *highest, middle and lowest*
169–72: now an A] *perhaps a reference to the queen, Anne of Bohemia*   makeles] *matchless, incomparable*

Hire goodly lokyng gladed al the prees.
Nas nevere yet seyn thyng to ben preysed derre,
Nor under cloude blak so bright a sterre   175

As was Criseyde, as folk seyde everichone
That hir behelden in hir blake wede;
And yet she stood ful lowe and stille allone,
Byhynden other folk, in litel brede,
And neigh the dore, ay undre shames drede,   180
Simple of atir, and debonaire of chere,
With ful assured lokyng and manere.

This Troilus, as he was wont to gide
His yonge knyghtes, lad hem up and down
In thilke large temple on every side,   185
Byholding ay the ladies of the town,
Now here, now there, for no devocioun
Hadde he to non, to reven hym his reste,
But gan to preise and lakken whom hym leste.

173–5: prees] *crowd*   preysed dere] *praised more highly*
176–82: everichone] *everyone*   hir blake wede] *her widow's weeds*   litel brede
small space   neigh the dore] *near the door*   shames drede] *fear of disgrace*
atir] *dress*   debonaire of chere] *gracious in style*
183–9: gide] *lead*   ay] *all the time*   devocioun] *commitment*   reven] *deprive*
lakken] *disparage*

And in his walk ful faste he gan to wayten   190
If knyght or squyer of his compaignie
Gan for to syke, or lete his eighen baiten
On any womman that he koude espye;
He wolde smyle, and holden it folye,
And seye hym thus, 'God woot, she slepeth softe   195
For love of the, whan thou turnest ful ofte!

'I have herd told, pardieux, of youre lyvynge,
Ye loveres, and your lewed observaunces,
And which a labour folk han in wynnynge
Of love, and, in the kepyng, which doutaunces;   200
And whan youre prey is lost, woo and penaunces;
O veray fooles! nyce and blynde be ye;
Ther nys nat oon kan war by other be.'

And with that word he gan caste up the browe,
Ascaunces, 'Loo! is this naught wisely spoken?'   205
At which the God of Love gan loken rowe
Right for despit, and shop for to ben wroken.

190–6: faste] *attentively*   wayten] *watch*   syke] *sigh*   baiten] *feast on*   woot]
knows   softe] *peacefully*   turnest] *toss*
197–203: pardieux] *by God*   lyvynge] *way of life*   lewed] *stupid*   labour]
trouble   doutaunces] *uncertainties*   veray] *real*   nyce] *stupid*
204–7: Ascaunces] *as if to say*   rowe] *angrily*   shop] *determined*   wroken]
avenged

57

He kidde anon his bowe nas naught broken;
For sodeynly he hitte hym atte fulle –
And yet as proud a pekok can he pulle.

O blynde world, O blynde entencioun!
How often falleth al the effect contraire
Of surquidrie and foul presumpcioun;
For kaught is proud, and kaught is debonaire.
This Troilus is clomben on the staire,   215
And litel weneth that he moot descenden.
But alday faileth thing that fooles wenden.

As proude Bayard gynneth for to skippe
Out of the weye, so pryketh hym his corn,
Til he a lasshe have of the longe whippe –   220
Than thynketh he, 'Though I praunce al byforn
First in the trays, ful fat and newe shorn,
Yet am I but an hors, and horses lawe
I moot endure, and with my feres drawe' –

208–10: kidde] *made known*   And yet] *so still*   pulle] *pluck*
211–17: entencioun] *intention*   falleth] *befalls*   surquidrie] *arrogance*
debonaire] *humble*   clomben] *climbed*   weneth] *thinks*
218–24: Bayard] *Charlemagne's horse*   gynneth] *starts*   pryketh] *urges,*
attracts   trays] *traces*   feres] *equals, fellows*

58

So ferde it by this fierse and proude knyght;　　225
Though he a worthy kynges sone were,
And wende nothing hadde had swich myght
Ayeyns his wille that shuld his herte stere,
Yet with a look his herte wex a-fere,
That he that now was moost in pride above,　　230
Wax sodeynly moost subgit unto love.

Forthy ensample taketh of this man,
Ye wise, proude, and worthi folkes alle,
To scornen Love, which that so soone can
The fredom of your hertes to hym thralle;　　235
For evere it was, and evere it shal byfalle,
That Love is he that alle thing may bynde;
For may no man fordon the lawe of kynde.

That this be soth, hath preved and doth yit.
For this trowe I ye knowen, alle or some,　　240
Men reden nat that folk han gretter wit
Than they that han be most with love ynome;

225–31: ferde] *happened*　stere] *control, disturb*　a-fere] *on fire*　subgit]
subjected
232–8: Forthy] *therefore*　To scornen] *about scorning*　thralle] *subject*
fordon] *overcome*
239–42: soth] *true*　preved] *been proved*　trowe] *believe*　alle or some]
everyone　reden] *judge*　ynome] *captured*

59

And strengest folk ben therwith overcome,
The worthiest and grettest of degree:
This was, and is, and yet men shal it see.   245

And trewelich it sit wel to be so,
For alderwisest han therwith ben plesed;
And they that han ben aldermost in wo,
With love han ben comforted moost and esed;
And ofte it hath the cruel herte apesed,   250
And worthi folk maad worthier of name,
And causeth moost to dreden vice and shame.

Now sith it may not goodly ben withstonde,
And is a thing so vertuous in kynde,
Refuseth not to Love for to ben bonde,   255
Syn, as hymselven liste, he may yow bynde.
The yerde is bet that bowen wole and wynde
Than that that brest; and therfore I yow rede
To folowen hym that so wel kan yow lede.

243–5: degree] *status*
246–52: sit] *is fitting*   alderwisest] *the wisest of all*   apesed] *appeased*   name]
reputation
253–9: goodly] *well*   kynde] *nature*   bonde] *enslaved*   liste] *chooses*   yerde]
stick   wynde] *bend*   brest] *breaks*   rede] *advise*

But for to tellen forth in special   260
Of this kynges sone of which I tolde,
And leten other thing collateral,
Of hym thenke I my tale forth to holde,
Both of his joie, and of his cares colde;
And al his werk, as touching this matere,   265
For I it gan, I wol therto refere.

Withinne the temple he wente hym forth pleyinge,
This Troilus, of every wight aboute,
On this lady and now on that lokynge,
Wher so she were of town or of without.   270
And upon cas bifel that thorugh a route
His eye percede, and so depe it wente,
Til on Criseyde it smot, and ther it stente.

And sodeynly he wax therwith astoned,
And gan hir bet biholde in thrifty wise: 275
'O mercy, God!' thoughte he, 'wher hastow woned,
That art so feyr and goodly to devise?'

260–6: collateral] *marginal*   holde] *keep to*   gan] *began*   refere] *return*
267–73: pleyinge . . . of] *joking with*   of town or of without] *from the town or outside it*   upon cas] *by chance*   stente] *halted*
274–7: astoned] *astonished*   bet] *more closely*   thrifty] *cautious*   woned] *lived*

Therwith his herte gan to sprede and rise,
And softe sighed, lest men myghte hym here,
And caughte ayeyn his firste pleyinge chere.   280

She nas nat with the leste of hire stature,
But alle hire lymes so wel answerynge
Weren to wommanhod, that creature
Was neuere lasse mannyssh in semynge.
And ek the pure wise of hire mevynge   285
Shewed wel that men myght in hire gesse
Honour, estat, and wommanly noblesse.

To Troilus right wonder wel with alle
Gan for to like hire mevynge and hire chere,
Which somdel deignous was, for she let falle   290
Hire look a lite aside, in swich manere,
Ascaunces, 'What! may I nat stonden here?'
And after that hir lokynge gan she lighte,
That nevere thoughte hym seen so good a syghte.

278–80: sprede] *expand*   pleyinge chere] *joking behaviour*
281–7: leste] *smallest*   answerynge] *conforming*   mannyssh] *masculine*
ek] *also*   pure wise] *very nature*   mevynge] *bearing*   gesse] *imagine*
288–94: wonder] *wonderfully*   with alle] *altogether*   somdel deignous] *a bit
haughty*   Ascaunces] *as if to say*   lighte] *radiate*

And of hire look in him ther gan to quyken   295
So gret desir and such affeccioun,
That in his herte botme gan to stiken
Of hir his fixe and depe impressioun.
And though he erst hadde poured up and down,
He was tho glad his hornes in to shrinke;   300
Unnethes wiste he how to loke or wynke.

Lo, he that leet hymselven so konnynge,
And scorned hem that Loves peynes dryen,
Was ful unwar that Love hadde his dwellynge
Withinne the subtile stremes of hir yen;   305
That sodeynly him thoughte he felte dyen,
Right with hir look, the spirit in his herte;
Blissed be Love, that kan thus folk converte!

She, this in blak, likynge to Troilus
Over alle thing, he stood for to biholde;   310
Ne his desir, ne wherfore he stood thus,
He neither chere made, ne word tolde;

295–301: of hire look] *from her glance*   quyken] *come to life*   herte botme]
heart's depth   fixe] *set*   poured] *gazed, pored*   tho] *then*   Unnethes] *hardly*
wynke] *close his eyes*
302–8: leet] *considered*   konnynge] *clever*   dryen] *endure*   unwar] *unaware*
subtile] *delicate*   yen] *eyes*   That] *so that*
309–12: likynge] *attractive*   chere made] *showed by his expression*

63

But from afer, his manere for to holde,
On other thing his look som tyme he caste,
And eft on hire, whil that servyse laste.   315

And after this, not fullich al awhaped,
Out of the temple al esilich he wente,
Repentynge hym that he hadde ever ijaped
Of Loves folk, lest fully the descente
Of scorn fille on hymself; but what he mente,   320
Lest it were wist on any manere syde,
His woo he gan dissimilen and hide.

Whan he was fro the temple thus departed,
He streght anon unto his paleys torneth,
Right with hire look thorugh-shoten and thorugh-darted,
                                                                          325

Al feyneth he in lust that he soiorneth;
And al his chere and speche also he borneth;
And ay, of Loves servants every while,
Hymself to wrye, at hem he gan to smyle,

313–15: manere] *disposition*
316–22: al awhaped] *entirely stunned*   esilich] *unhurriedly*   ijaped/Of]
mocked at   mente] *thought*
323–9: thorugh-darted] *pierced through*   lust] *pleasure*   soiorneth] *continues*
borneth] *polishes*   wrye] *hide*

And seyde, 'Lord, so ye lyve al in lest,   330
Ye loveres! For the konnyngeste of yow,
That serveth most ententiflich and best,
Hym tit as often harm therof as prow;
Your hire is quyt ayeyn, ye, God woot how!
Nought wel for wel, but scorn for good servyse;   335
In feith, your ordre is ruled in good wise!

'In nouncerteyn ben alle your observaunces,
But it a sely fewe pointes be;
Ne no thing asketh so grete attendaunces
As doth youre lay, and that knowe alle ye;   340
But that is nat the worste, as mote I the!
But, tolde I yow the worste point, I leve,
Al seyde I soth, ye wolden at me greve!

'But take this, that ye loveres ofte eschuwe,
Or elles doon of good entencioun,   345
Ful ofte thi lady wole it mysconstruwe,
And deme it harm in hire oppynyoun;

330-6: lest] *happiness*   ententiflich] *assiduously*   Hym tit] *it befalls him*
prow] *benefit*   hire] *payment*   quyt] *requited*   woot] *knows*   ordre] *religion*
337-43: nouncerteyn] *uncertainty*   But it] *except*   sely] *insignificant*
attendaunces] *attention*   lay] *faith*   the] *prosper*   leve] *believe*   Al] *even if*
greve] *complain*
344-7: that] *what*   eschuwe] *avoid*

And yet if she, for other enchesoun,
Be wroth, than shaltow han a groyn anon.
Lord! wel is hym that may ben of yow oon!'   350

But for al this, whan that he say his tyme,
He held his pees – non other boote hym gayned –
For love bigan his fetheres so to lyme,
That wel unnethe until his folk he fayned
That other besy nedes hym destrayned;   355
For wo was hym, that what to doon he nyste,
But bad his folk to gon wher that hem liste.

And whan that he in chambre was allone,
He doun upon his beddes feet him sette,
And first he gan to sike, and eft to grone,   360
And thought ay on hire so, withouten lette,
That, as he sat and wook, his spirit mette
That he hir saw a-temple, and al the wise
Right of hire look, and gan it newe avise.

348–50: enchesoun] *reason*   groyn] *complaint*
351-7: say] *saw*   boote hym gayned] *was any help to him*   lyme] *smear with*
quicklime (to trap him)   unnethe] *hardly*   until his folk] *to his friends*
destrayned] *preoccupied*   wo was hym] *'he was very sorry, but . . .'*   nyste] *did*
not know   wher that hem liste] *wherever they pleased*
358–64: sike] *sigh*   eft] *then*   lette] *pause*   wook] *was awake*   mette] *dreamed*
a-temple] *in the temple*   wise] *nature*   avise] *bring to mind*

66

Thus gan he make a mirour of his mynde, 365
In which he saugh al holly hire figure;
And that he wel koude in his herte fynde,
It was to hym a right good aventure
To love swich oon, and if he dede his cure
To serven hir, yet myghte he falle in grace, 370
Or elles for oon of hir servantz pace.

Imagenynge that travaille nor grame
Ne myghte for so goodly oon be lorn
As she, ne hym for his desir no shame,
Al were it wist, but in pris and up-born 375
Of alle lovers wel more than biforn;
Thus argumented he in his gynnynge,
Ful unavysed of his woo comynge.

Thus took he purpos loves craft to suwe,
And thoughte he wolde werken pryvely, 380
First to hiden his desir in muwe
From every wight y-born, al outrely,

365–71: al holly] *completely*   that] *what*   aventure] *experience*   dede his cure]
took pains   falle in grace] *have good fortune*   pace] *pass for*
372–8: travaille] *labour*   grame] *suffering*   lorn] *wasted*   Al were it wist] *even
if it became known*   pris] *esteem*   up-born] *admired*   gynnynge] *start*
unavysed] *unaware*   comynge] *to come*
379–82: suwe] *follow*   in muwe] *in secret (like a caged hawk)*   outrely]
completely

But he myghte ought recovered be therby,
Remembryng hym that love to wyde yblowe
Yelt bittre fruyt, though swete seed be sowe.   385

And over al this, yet muchel more he thoughte
What for to speke, and what to holden inne;
And what to arten hir to love he soughte,
And on a song anon-right to bygynne,
And gan loude on his sorwe for to wynne;   390
For with good hope he gan fully assente
Criseyde for to love, and nought repente.

And of his song naught only the sentence,
As writ myn auctour called Lollius,
But pleinly, save our tonges difference,   395
I dar wel seyn in al that Troilus
Seyde in his song, loo, every word right thus
As I shal seyn; and whoso list it here,
Loo, next this vers he may it finden here.

383–5: But] *lest*   yblowe] *broadcast*   Yelt] *yields*   sowe] *sown*
386–92: arten] *prompt*   wynne] *overcome*   repente] *regret*
393–9: sentence] *meaning*   writ] *writes*   auctour] *authority*   Lollius] *(the invented author Chaucer pretends to be translating)*   in al] *entirely*
list] *wants to*

Canticus Troili

'If no love is, O God, what fele I so?   400
And if love is, what thing and which is he!
If love be good, from whennes cometh my woo?
If it be wikke, a wonder thynketh me,
When every torment and adversite
That cometh of hym may to me savory thinke,   405
For ay thurst I, the more that ich it drynke.

'And if that at myn owen lust I brenne,
Fro whennes cometh my waillynge and my pleynte?
If harm agree me, wherto pleyne I thenne?
I noot, ne whi unwery that I feynte.   410
O quike deeth, O swete harm so queynte,
How may of the in me swich quantite,
But if that I consente that it be?

'And if that I consente, I wrongfully
Compleyne, iwis. Thus possed to and fro,   415

Canticus Troili: 'Troilus' song' – what follows is Chaucer's skilful adaptation into his seven-lined rhyme-royal stanzas of the fourteen lines of a sonnet by Petrarch (Rime CXXXII).
400–6: is] *exists*   wikke] *evil*   savory] *delicious*
407–13: lust] *inclination*   brenne] *burn*   pleynte] *complaint*   agree me] *agrees with me*   wherto] *why*   noot] *don't know*   unwery] *without being tired*   quike deeth] *living deeth*   queynte] *strange*   may] *can there be*
414–15: possed] *tossed*

Al sterelees withinne a boot am I
Amydde the see, bitwixen wyndes two,
That in contrarie stonden evere mo.
Allas! what is this wondre maladie?
For hete of cold, for cold of hete, I dye.'   420

After Troilus' lamentations (ending here with the version of a
Petrarch sonnet), he declares in private his devotion to the absent
Criseyde and is inspired by it to great deeds of arms. After much
lover's lamentation, he is persuaded by his friend Pandarus (himself
an unsuccessful lover) to reveal the name of the lady who causes
his woe. On hearing that it is Criseyde, Pandarus undertakes to
intercede for Troilus with this wise, gracious and worthy lady who
is his niece. Reassured, Troilus becomes 'the frendlieste wight, the
gentileset, and ek the moste fre [noble]' (1079–80).

Book 2 begins with one of the poem's two great prologues, both
additions by Chaucer to his source in Boccaccio. Opening with lines
that echo Dante's *Purgatorio*, Chaucer describes the improvement
in Troilus' circumstances in somewhat unreassuring and relative
terms:

416–20: sterelees] *rudderless*

Owt of thise blake wawes for to saylle,
O wynd, O wynd, the weder gynneth clere;
For in this see the boot hath swych travaylle
Of my connyng, that unneth I it steere.
This see clepe I the tempestous matere   5
Of disespeyr that Troilus was inne:
But now of hope the kalendes bygynne.

O lady myn, that called art Cleo,
Thou be my speed fro this forth, and my Muse,
To ryme wel this book til I have do;   10
Me nedeth here noon other art to use:
Forwhi to every lovere I me excuse,
That of no sentement I this endite,
But out of Latyn in my tonge it write.

Wherfore I nyl have neither thank ne blame   15
Of al this werk, but prey yow mekely,
Disblameth me if any word be lame,
For as myn auctour seyde, so sey I.

1–7: wawes] *waves*   gynneth clere] *begins to clear up*   boot ... Of my connyng]
boat of my wit (cf. Dante's '*la navicella del mio ingegno*', *Purgatorio*, 1, 2)
travaylle] *difficulty*   unneth] *hardly*   steere] *steer*   clepe] *call*   kalendes] *first
day of the month (start)*
8–14: Cleo] *Clio, the Muse of History*   speed] *cause of success*   noon other art]
i.e. except History   Forwhi] *wherefore*   sentement] *emotional insight*   Latyn]
i.e. the language of Chaucer's invented source, Lollius
15–18: nyl] *don't want to*   Disblameth] *excuse*

Ek though I speeke of love unfelyngly,
No wondre is, for it nothyng of newe is;   20
A blynd man can nat juggen wel in hewis.

Ye knowe ek that in forme of speche is chaunge
Withinne a thousand yeer, and wordes tho
That hadden pris, now wonder nyce and straunge
Us thinketh hem; and yet they spake hem so,   25
And spedde as wel in love as men now do;
Ek for to wynnen love in sondry ages,
In sondry londes, sondry ben usages.

And forthi if it happe in any wyse,
That here be any lovere in this place   30
That herkneth, as the storie wol devise,
How Troilus com to his lady grace,
And thenketh, 'So nold I nat love purchace',
Or wondreth on his speche or his doynge,
I noot; but it is me no wonderynge;   35

For every wight which that to Rome went
Halt nat o path, or alwey o manere;
Ek in som lond were al the game shent,
If that they ferde in love as men don here,
As thus, in opyn doyng or in chere,   40
In visityng in forme, or seyde hire sawes;
Forthi men seyn, 'Ecch contree hath his lawes'.

Ek scarsly ben ther in this place thre
That have in love seid lik and don in al;
For to thi purpos this may liken the,   45
And the right nought, yet al is seid or schal;
Ek som men grave in tree, some in ston wal,
As it bitit. But syn I have bigonne,
Myn auctour shal I folwen, if I konne.

After the prologue we find Pandarus lovelorn while a swallow sings
her 'sorrowful lay' outside his window, before making his way to
meet Criseyde, whom he finds reading the grim story of the *Siege of*

36–42: wight] *person*   went (wendeth)] *goes*   Halt (haldeth)] *holds, keeps to*
o] *the same*   shent] *lost*   ferde] *acted*   As thus] *such as*   opyn doyng] *acting*
in public   chere] *conduct*   in forme] *formally*   sawes] *words*
43–9: in al] *entirely*   liken] *appeal to*   the . . . the] *someone . . . someone else*
schal] *will happen*   grave] *carve, write*   bitit] *betides, happens*

Thebes in which the Bishop Amphiorax 'fell through the ground to Hell' (105). He tells her that Troilus – 'the good, wise, worthy, fresh and free' – loves her (317). After Pandarus leaves, Criseyde hears admiring shouts from the street and looks out to see Troilus on his bay steed riding past. She observes his noble bearing, and 'leet it so softe into her herte synke / That to herself she said "Who yaf me drynke!"' (650–1): who has plied her with an irresistible love potion like Tristan's? On her own she ponders what to do: she is her 'owene woman', at liberty, to whom no husband can say 'Chek mat!' (750–4); love is a stormy life. She joins her three nieces in the garden, and one of them, Antigone, sings a song in praise of love, written by 'the goodlieste mayde / Of gret estat in al the towns of Troye' (880–1). That night she dreams that her heart was torn out painlessly by an egle 'fethered whit as bon [ivory]' (925). The next day Troilus at the end of his feats of arms sends for Pandarus who 'came leaping in at once' (939) and proposes that he and Criseyde will watch Troilus riding past the next day. In addition Troilus writes her a letter, sealed with the ruby in his signet, bathed with salt tears. Pandarus delivers the letter to Criseyde, and sets about getting Criseyde to the window to watch: these exchanges between the uncle and niece are some of the most modern-seeming and colloquially inventive things in the whole of Chaucer.

Tho wesshen they, and sette hem down and ete;
And after noon ful sleighly Pandarus   1185
Gan drawe him to the window next the strete,
And seyde, 'Nece, who hath araied thus
The yonder hous, that stant aforyeyn us?'
'Which hous?' quod she, and gan for to byholde,
And knew it wel, and whos it was hym tolde;   1190

And fillen forth in speche of thynges smale,
And seten in the window bothe tweye.
Whan Pandarus saugh tyme unto his tale,
And saugh wel that hire folk were alle aweye,
'Now, nece myn, tel on,' quod he; 'I seye,   1195
How liketh yow the lettre that he wrot?
Kan he ther-on? For, by my trouthe, I noot.'

Therwith al rosy hewed tho wex she,
And gan to homme, and seyde, 'So I trowe.'
'Aquite him wel, for Goddes love,' quod he;   1200
'Myself to medes wol the lettre sowe.'

1184–90: wesshen] *wash*   sleighly] *cunningly*   next] *nearest*   araied] *decorated*
aforyeyn] *in front of*
1191–7: fillen forth] *fill up*   smale] *trivial*   seten] *sit*   tyme] *opportunity*
folk] *household*   woot] *know about*   Kan he ther-on?] *does he know about
things?*   noot] *don't know*
1198–201: wex] *became*   homme] *hum*   trowe] *think*   Aquite] *repay*   to
medes] *as a contribution*   sowe] *sew up (the letter)*

And held his hondes up, and sat on knowe;
'Now, goode nece, be it nevere so lite,
Yif me the labour it to sowe and plite.'

'Ye, for I can so writen,' quod she tho;   1205
'And ek I noot what I sholde to hym seye.'
'Nay, nece,' quod Pandare, 'sey nat so;
Yet at the leste thonketh him, I preye,
Of his good wille, and doth him not to deye.
Now for the love of me, my nece deere,   1210
Refuseth nat at this tid my prayere.'

'Depardieux,' quod she, 'God leve al be wel!
God help me so, this is the firste lettre
That evere I wroot, ye, al or any del.'
And into a closet, for to avise hire bettre,   1215
She wente allone, and gan hire herte unfettre
Out of desdaynes prisoun but a lite;
And sette hire down, and gan a lettre write,

1202–4: knowe] *knee (knelt down?)*   lite] *little*   plite] *fold*
1205–11: ek] *yet*   thonketh] *thank*   Of his] *for his*   doth him not to deye] *don't cause him to die*   tid] *time*
1212–18: Depardieux] *by God*   leve] *let it*   any del] *any bit*   avise] *concentrate*
desdaynes] *reserve's*

Of which to telle in short is myn entente
Theffect, as fer as I kan understonde.   1220
She thanked him of al that he wel mente
Towardes hire, but holden hym in honde
She nolde nought, ne make hireselven bonde
In love; but as his suster, hym to plese,
She wolde fayn to doon his herte an ese.   1225

She shette it, and to Pandarus in gan goon,
Ther as he sat and loked into the strete,
And down she sette hire by hym on a stoon
Of jaspre, upon a quysshyn gold ybete,
And seyde, 'As wisly helpe me god the grete,   1230
I never dide a thing with more peyne
Than writen this, to which ye me constreyne',

And took it hym. He thonked hire and seyde,
'God woot, of thyng ful often looth bygonne
Comth ende good; and nece myn, Criseyde,   1235
That ye to hym of hard now ben ywonne

1219–25: holden hym in honde] *coax him*   bonde] *committed*   as his suster]
like a sister   wolde fayn] *would like*
1226–32: shette it] *shut it up*   quysshyn] *cushion*   constreyne] *oblige*
1233–6: looth] *reluctantly*   of hard] *with difficulty*

Oughte he be glad, by God and yonder sonne!
Forwhi men seith, "Impressiounes lighte
Ful lightly ben ay redy to the flighte."

'But ye han pleyed tirant neigh to longe,   1240
And hard was it youre herte for to grave.
Now stynt, that ye no lenger on it honge,
Al wolde ye the forme of daunger save,
But hasteth you to doon him joye have;
For trusteth wel, to long ydoon hardnesse   1245
Causeth despit ful often for destresse.'

And right as they declamed this matere,
Lo, Troilus, right at the stretes ende,
Com ryding with his tenthe some yfere,
Al softely, and thiderward gan bende   1250
Ther as they sete, as was his way to wende
To paleis-ward; and Pandare him aspide,
And seyde, 'Nece, ysee who comth here ride!

1237–9: lightly] *easily*
1240–6: neigh] *nearly*   grave] *engrave (with Troilus' image)*   honge] *stay
undecided*   Al wolde ye] *even though you'd like*   forme of daunger save]
maintain the impression of reserve   hardnesse] *resistance*   despit] *bitterness*
1247–53: declamed] *talked about*   tenthe some yfere] *along with his party*
often   softely] *unostentatiously*   way] *route*   wende] *travel*

'O fle naught in (he seeth us, I suppose)
Lest he may thynken that ye hym eschuwe.'   1255
'Nay, nay,' quod she, and wex as red as rose.
With that he gan hire humbly to saluwe
With dredful chere, and oft his hewes muwe;
And up his look debonairly he caste,
And bekked on Pandare, and forth he paste.   1260

God woot if he sat on his hors aright
Or goodly was biseyn that ilke day!
God woot wher he was lik a manly knyght!
What sholde I drecche, or telle of his aray?
Criseyde, which that alle these thynges say,   1265
To telle in short, hire lyked al in-fere,
His persoun, his aray, his look, his chere,

His goodly manere, and his gentilesse,
So wel that nevere, sith that she was born,
Ne hadde she swych routh of his destresse;   1270
And how so she hath hard ben here-byforn,

1254–60: suppose] *imagine*   eschuwe] *avoid*   saluwe] *salute*   dredful chere]
fearful demeanour   hewes muwe] *complexion changes*   debonairly] *graciously*
bekked on] *nodded at*
1261–7: God woot] *God alone knows*   biseyn] *looking*   ilke] *same*   wher]
whether   drecche] *delay*   say] *saw*   in-fere] *all round*   chere] *manner*
1268–71: gentilesse] *courtly nobility*   sith] *since*   hard] *unyielding*

To God hope I, she hath now kaught a thorn,
She shal nat pulle it out this nexte wyke;
God sende mo swich thornes on to pike!

Pandare, which that stood hire faste by,   1275
Felte iren hoot, and he bygan to smyte,
And seyde, 'Nece, I pray yow hertely,
Tel me that I shal axen yow a lite:
A womman, that were of his deth to wite,
Withouten his gilt, but for hir lakked routhe,   1280
Were it wel doon?' Quod she, 'Nay, by my trouthe!'

'God help me so,' quod he, 'ye sey me soth.
Ye felen wel youreself that I nought lye;
Lo, yond he rit!' Quod she, 'Ye, so he doth!'
'Wel,' quod Pandare, 'as I have told yow thrie,   1285
Lat be youre nyce shame and youre folie,
And spek with him in esyng of his herte;
Lat nycete nat do yow bothe smerte.'

1272–4: hope I] *I think*   wyke] *week*   pike] *pick*
1275–81: faste] *close*   smyte] *strike*   that] *what*   a lite] *briefly*   wite] *know*
for hir] *because she*   routhe] *pity*
1282–8: rit] *rides*   thrie] *three times*   nyce] *foolish*   nycete] *stupidity*   do yow
. . . smerte] *cause you pain*

But theron was to heven and to doone;
Considered al thing it may not be;   1290
And whi? For speche; and it were ek to soone
To graunten hym so gret a libertee.
For pleynly hire entente, as seyde she,
Was for to love hym unwist, if she myghte,
And guerdoun hym with nothing but with sighte.   1295

But Pandarus thought, 'It shal nought be so,
Yif that I may; this nyce opynyoun
Shal nought be holden fully yeres two.'
What sholde I make of this a long sermoun?
He moste assente on that conclusioun,   1300
As for the tyme; and whan that it was eve,
And al was wel, he roos and tok his leve.

And on his wey ful faste homward he spedde,
And right for joye he felte his herte daunce;
And Troilus he fond allone abedde,   1305
That lay as do thise lovers, in a traunce,

1289–95: theron] *to that end*   to heven and to doone] *effort and action to be done*   Considered] *think of*   speche] *gossip*   entente] *intention*   unwist] *secretly*   guerdoun] *reward*
1296–302: I may] *have anything to do with it*   nyce opynyoun] *foolish intention*   What] *why*   sermoun] *story*   assente on] *agree to*   As for the tyme] *for the time being*
1303–6: spedde] *hurried*

81

Bitwixen hope and derk disesperaunce.
But Pandarus, right at his in-comynge,
He song, as who seyth, 'Lo! Sumwhat I brynge,'

And seyde, 'Who is in his bed so soone   1310
Iburied thus?' 'It am I, freend,' quod he.
'Who, Troilus? Nay, help me so the Moone!'
Quod Pandarus, 'Thow shalt arise and see
A charme that was sent right now to the,
The which kan helen the of thyn accesse,   1315
If thow do forthwith al thi bisynesse.'

After this meeting with Criseyde, Pandarus sets about his machina-
tions, beginning with a rather elaborate scheme (new in Chaucer)
involving a party at the house of Troilus' favourite brother Deiphe-
bus, attended by Hector, Troilus, Paris and Helen as well as Criseyde
and her nieces. Pandarus puts Troilus to bed at the party, saying that
he is ill (which in a way he is, with love-sickness) and persuades
Criseyde to visit his sickbed. Book 2 ends with Troilus in bed,
listening to Pandarus and Criseyde whispering next door.

1307–9: song] *sang*
1310–16: help me so the Moone!] *the Moon help me!*   charme] *lucky charm*
accesse] *fever*   bisynesse] *duty*

This scheme is left in soap-opera suspension while the second of the great prologues follows, the hymn to Venus, goddess of love, at the start of Book 3. Criseyde and Troilus agree the terms of their love before they part: though Troilus is a king's son, Criseyde says he will not have 'sovereignete of me in love' (171–2). In conversation with Troilus, Pandarus worries that he may have a bad name as 'such a meene / as maketh women unto men to comen' (254–5), and he urges Troilus to protect Criseyde's good name by secrecy. To assure him of the acceptability of his encouragement of love, Troilus (rather disturbingly to us) offers to reciprocate by fixing up any of his sisters – or even Helen herself – with Pandarus (409–10). Pandarus carries letters between the lovers, and then devises his second major scheme to facilitate the consummation of their love. He invites Criseyde to dinner at his house, and she, along with her entourage of women, is held there by a night of extraordinary rain. Criseyde goes to bed, and is persuaded at length by Pandarus of the necessity to put to rest the fears of Troilus (who happens to be in the house) because some tale-bearer has told him that Criseyde is in love with someone called Horaste. Finally Troilus is brought to her bedside for reassurance and the consummation follows once Pandarus has thrown him into bed and stripped him to his shirt. Despite all this, the long climactic scene is described with great lyricism.

This Troilus, with blisse of that supprised,
Put al in Goddes hond, as he that mente   1185
Nothing but wel; and, sodeynly avysed,
He hire in armes faste to hym hente.
And Pandarus, with a ful good entente,
Leyde hym to slepe, and seyde, 'If ye be wise,
Swouneth nought now, lest more folk arise.'   1190

What myghte or may the sely larke seye
Whan that the sperhauk hath it in his foot?
I kan namore, but of thise ilke tweye –
To whom this tale sucre be or soot –
Though that I tarie a yer, somtyme I moot,   1195
After myn auctour, tellen hire gladnesse,
As wel as I have told hir hevynesse.

Criseyde, which that felte hire thus itake,
As writen clerkes in hir bokes olde,
Right as an aspes leef she gan to quake,   1200
Whan she hym felte hire in his armes folde.

<hr>

1184–90: supprised] *affected*   avysed] *determined*   hente] *seized*   Leyde] *set
about*   Swouneth] *faint*   arise] *get up (and disturb you)*
1191–7: sely] *innocent*   sperhauk] *sparrowhawk*   soot] *soot (i.e. bitter)*   moot]
must   After] *following*
1198–201: itake] *captured*   clerkes] *writers*   aspes] *aspen's*   folde] *embrace*

But Troilus, al hool of cares colde,
Gan thanken tho the bryghte goddes sevene;
Thus sondry peynes bryngen folk in hevene.

This Troilus in armes gan hire streyne,   1205
And seyde, 'O swete, as ever mot I gon,
Now be ye kaught, now is ther but we tweyne;
Now yeldeth yow, for other bote is non.'
To that Criseyde answerde thus anon,
'Ne hadde I er now, my swete herte deere,   1210
Ben yolde, ywis, I were now nought here!'

O! sooth is seyd, that heled for to be
As of a fevre or othere gret siknesse,
Men moste drynke, as men may ofte se,
Ful bittre drynke; and for to han gladnesse   1215
Men drynken ofte peyne and gret distresse;
I mene it here, as for this aventure,
That thorugh a peyne hath founden al his cure.

1202–4: al hool of] *entirely cured of*   goddes sevene] *seven planetary gods*
sondry] *various*
1205–11: streyne] *squeeze*   gon] *succeed*   bote] *cure*   yolde] *given up (by
herself)*
1212–18: heled] *cured*

And now swetnesse semeth more swete,
That bitternesse assaied was byforn;   1220
For out of wo in blisse now they flete;
Non swich they felten, sithen they were born.
Now is this bet than bothe two be lorn.
For love of God, take every womman heede
To werken thus, if it comth to the neede.   1225

Criseyde, al quyt from every drede and tene,
As she that juste cause hadde hym to triste,
Made hym swych feste it joye was to sene,
Whan she his trouthe and clene entente wiste.
And as aboute a tree, with many a twiste,   1230
Bytrent and writh the swote wodebynde,
Gan ech of hem in armes other wynde.

And as the newe abaysed nyghtyngale,
That stynteth first whan she bygynneth to synge
Whan that she hereth any herde tale,   1235
Or in the hegges any wyght stirynge,

1219–25: That] *because*   assaied] *tried*   flete] *float*   sithen] *since*   lorn] *lost*
1226–32: quyt] *freed*   tene] *pain*   clene] *honourable*   Bytrent] *encircles*
writh] *twists*   swote] *sweet*   wodebynde] *woodbine*
1233–6: newe abaysed] *suddenly startled*   stynteth] *stops*   herde] *shepherd*
tale] *talk*   any wyght] *anybody*   stirynge] *moving*

And after siker doth hire vois out rynge,
Right so Criseyde, whan hire drede stente,
Opned hir herte and tolde hym hire entente.

And right as he that seth his deth yshapen,   1240
And dyen mot, in ought that he may gesse,
And sodeynly rescous doth him escapen,
And from his deth is brought in sykernesse,
For al this world, in swych present gladnesse
Was Troilus, and hath his lady swete;   1245
With worse hap God lat us nevere mete!

Hire armes smale, hir streghte bak, and softe,
Hire sydes longe, flesshly, smothe, and white
He gan to stroke, and good thrift bad ful ofte
Hire snowissh throte, hire brestes rounde and lite.   1250
Thus in this hevene he gan hym to delite,
And therwithal a thousand tyme hire kiste,
That what to don for joye unnethe he wiste.

1237–9: siker] *secure*
1240–6: yshapen] *imminent*   in ought that] *as far as*   rescous] *rescue*
escapen] *set free*   sykernesse] *safety*
1247–53: smale] *slender*   flesshly] *shapely*   thrift] *success (in praise)*
snowissh] *snow-white*   unnethe] *hardly*

Than seyde he thus, 'O Love, O Charite!
Thi moder ek, Citheria the swete,   1255
After thiself next heried be she –
Venus mene I, the wel-willy planete! –
And next that, Imeneus, I the grete,
For nevere man was to yow goddes holde
As I, which ye han brought fro cares colde.   1260

'Benigne Love, thow holy bond of thynges,
Whoso wol grace and list the nought honouren,
Lo, his desir wol fle withouten wynges;
For noldestow of bownte hem socouren
That serven best and most alwey labouren,   1265
Yet were al lost, that dar I wel seyn, certes,
But if thi grace passed oure desertes.

'And for thow me, that koude leest disserve
Of hem that noumbred ben unto thi grace,
Hast holpen, ther I likly was to sterve,   1270
And me bistowed in so heigh a place

1254–60: Citheria] *Venus (mother of the god of love, apostrophised in the Prologue
to Book 3)* heried] *praised* wel-willy] *benevolent* Imeneus] *Hymen, the god
of marriage*
1261–7: wol] *wants* noldestow] *if you're not willing* socouren] *help* grace]
generosity
1268–71: for] *because* noumbred] *counted* grace] *favoured by you* ther]
where sterve] *die*

That thilke boundes may no blisse pace,
I kan namore, but laude and reverence
Be to thy bounte and thyn excellence!'

And therwithal Criseyde anon he kiste,   1275
Of which certein she felte no disese,
And thus seyde he: 'Now wolde God I wiste,
Myn herte swete, how I yow myght plese!
What man,' quod he, 'was evere thus at ese
As I, on which the faireste and the beste   1280
That ever I say deyneth hire herte reste.

'Here may men seen that mercy passeth right;
Th'experience of that is felt in me,
That am unworthi to so swete a wight.
But herte myn, of your benignite,   1285
So thynketh, though that I unworthi be,
Yet mot I nede amenden in som wyse,
Right thorugh the vertu of youre heigh servyse.

'And for the love of God, my lady deere,
Syn God hath wrought me for I shall yow serve –   1290
As thus I mene: he wol ye be my steere,
To do me lyve, if that yow liste, or sterve –
So techeth me how that I may disserve
Youre thonk, so that I thorugh myn ignoraunce
Ne do no thyng that yow be displesaunce.   1295

'For certes, fresshe wommanliche wif,
This dar I seye, that trouth and diligence,
That shal ye fynden in me al my lyf;
N'y wol not, certein, breken youre defence;
And if I do, present or in absence,   1300
For love of God, lat sle me with the dede,
If that it like unto youre wommanhede.'

The narrator declares his inadequacy to describe the bliss these lovers
experience (1337). They wonder if they are dreaming, and then they
exchange rings, symbolising the superiority of love over avarice (1400).

And evere mo, when that hem fel to speke
Of any wo of swich a tyme agoon,
With kissyng al that tale sholde breke,

1289–95: for I shall] *in order that I should*   steere] *guide*   do me lyve ... or
sterve] *cause me to live or die*
1296–302: wommanliche] *feminine*   defence] *prohibition*   lat sle me] *let me be
slain*
1401–3: hem fel] *they happened*   breke] *interrupt*

And fallen in a newe joye anoon,
And diden al hire myght, syn they were oon,   1405
For to recoveren blisse and ben at eise,
And passed wo with joie contrepeise.

Resoun wol nought that I speke of slep,
For it accordeth nought to my matere;
God woot, they took of that ful litel kep!   1410
But lest this nyght, that was to hem so deere,
Ne sholde in veyn escape in no manere,
It was byset in joie and bisynesse
Of al that souneth into gentilesse.

But whan the cok, comune astrologer,   1415
Gan on his brest to bete and after crowe,
And Lucyfer, the dayes messager,
Gan for to rise, and out hire bemes throwe;
And estward roos – to him that koude it knowe –
Fortuna maior, that anoon Criseyde,   1420
With herte sore, to Troilus thus seyde:

1404–7: oon] *alone*   passed] *past*   contrepeise] *counterbalance*
1408–14: matere] *subject*   in no manere] *in any way*   byset] *spent*
1415–21: comune astrologer] *universal astronomer*   Lucyfer] *the morning star,
Venus*   Fortuna maior] *an obscure constellation or planet*

'Myn hertes lif, my trist and my plesaunce,
That I was born, allas, what me is wo,
That day of us moot make disseveraunce!
For tyme it is to ryse and hennes go,   1425
Or ellis I am lost for evere mo!
O nyght, allas, why nyltow over us hove
As longe as whan Almena lay by Jove?

'O blake nyght, as folk in bokes rede,
That shapen art by God this world to hide   1430
At certeyn tymes wyth thy derke wede,
That under that men myghte in reste abide,
Wel oughten bestes pleyne and folk thee chide,
That there as day wyth labour wolde us breste,
That thow thus fleest, and deynest us nought reste. 1435

'Thow doost, allas, to shortly thyn office,
Thow rakle nyght! Ther God, maker of kynde,
The, for thyn haste and thyn unkynde vice,
So faste ay to oure hemysperie bynde

1422–8: what me is wo] *how I regret*   hove] *hover*   Almena] *Alcmena, the*
mother of Hercules. Jupiter extended the night so that she could conceive Hercules
with him
1429–35: wede] *clothing*   bestes] *animals*   there as] *when*   breste] *afflict*
deynest] *grant*
1436–9: shortly] *briefly*   office] *duty*   rakle] *hasty*   Ther God] *may*
God   kynde] *Nature*   unkynde] *unnatural*   faste] *firmly*   hemysperie]
overground hemisphere

That never more under the ground thow wynde!   1440
For now, for thow so hiest out of Troie,
Have I forgon thus hastili my joie!'

This Troilus, that with tho wordes felte,
As thoughte hym tho, for pietous distresse
The blody teris from his herte melte,   1445
As he that nevere yet swich hevynesse
Assayed hadde, out of so gret gladnesse,
Gan therwithal Criseyde, his lady deere,
In armes streyne, and seyde in this manere:

'O cruel day, accusour of the joie   1450
That nyght and love han stole and faste iwryen,
Acorsed be thi comyng into Troye,
For every bore hath oon of thi bryghte yen!
Envyous day, what list the so to spien?
What hastow lost? Why sekestow this place,   1455
Ther god thi light so quenche, for his grace!

1440-2: wynde] *turn*   for thow so hiest] *because you hasten so*
1443-9: tho] *then*   pietous] *pitiful*   Assayed] *experienced*   out of] *in exchange for*   streyne] *squeeze*
1450-6: accusour] *prosecutor*   iwryen] *hidden*   bore] *opening*   yen] *eyes*
what list the] *why do you want*   spien] *search*

93

'Allas, what han thise loveris the agylt,
Dispitous day? Thyn be the pyne of helle!
For many a lovere hastow slayn, and wilt;
Thy pouring in wol nowher lat hem dwelle.   1460
What profrestow thi light here for to selle?
Go selle it hem that smale selys grave;
We wol the nought; us nedeth no day have.'

And ek the sonne, Titan gan, he chide,
And seyde, 'O fool, wel may men the dispise,   1465
That hast the dawyng al nyght by thi syde,
And suffrest hire so soone up fro the rise
For to disese loveris in this wyse.
What, holde youre bed ther, thow, and ek thi Morwe!
I bidde God, so yeve yow bothe sorwe!'   1470

After this passionate aubade, the lovers part. Pandarus meets both
lovers and carries on facilitating their meetings. Troilus is made
virtuous by love, both in his general demeanour and in martial
exploits. 'But al to litel, weylaway the while, / Lasteth swich joie,
ythonked be Fortune', is the start of the prologue to Book 4: 'all

1457–63: what han] *how have*   agylt] *offended*   Dispitous] *merciless*   peyne]
pain   pouring] *staring*   What profrestow] *why do you offer*   selle] *sell*   smale
selys grave] *engrave small seals (in the Mint, which needs good light: cf. Donne's
'Sonne Rising')*
1464–70: Titan] *(confused with Tithonus, the lover of Aurora, the
Dawn)*   dawyng] *dawn, Aurora*   disese] *disturb*   Morwe] *the dawn*

too briefly, alas, lasts such joy, thanks to Fortune'. Calchas, the soothsayer who is Criseyde's father, foresees (correctly) the fall of Troy and persuades the Greeks to trade the Trojan prisoner-of-war Antenor (who will betray Troy) for his daughter. Troilus and Criseyde are distraught; Pandarus persuades Troilus to try to run away with Criseyde, but she refuses, full of fear as she is. The weakest part of the poem is the long interpolation on Free Will put into Troilus' mouth (974–1078); at the end of it, Troilus and Criseyde argue about what to do, and Criseyde undertakes to return from the Greek camp within ten days. Book 5, which is the poem's great triumph as it follows the 'fatal destinee / That Joves hath in disposicioun' (1–2), begins with the departure of Criseyde into the hands of Diomede, a plausible Greek lover. Back in Troy, Troilus suffers from terrible nightmares.

> And whan he fil in any slomberynges,
> Anon bygynne he sholde for to grone,
> And dremen of the dredefulleste thynges
> That myghte ben; as mete he were allone
> In place horrible makyng ay his mone, 250
> Or meten that he was amonges alle
> His enemys, and in hire hondes falle.

246–52: slomberynges] *slumber*   as mete] *such as to dream*

And therwithal his body sholde sterte,
And with the stert al sodeynliche awake,
And swich a tremour fele aboute his herte,   255
That of the fere his body sholde quake;
And therwithal he sholde a noyse make,
And seme as though he sholde falle depe
From heighe o-lofte; and thanne he wolde wepe,

And rewen on hymself so pitously,   260
That wonder was to here his fantasie.
Another tyme he sholde myghtyly
Conforte hymself, and sein it was folie
So causeles swich drede for to drye,
And eft bygynne his aspre sorwes newe,   265
That every man myght on his sorwes rewe.

Who koude telle aright or ful discryve
His wo, his pleynt, his langour, and his pyne?
Naught alle the men that han or ben on lyve.
Thow, redere, mayst thiself ful wel devyne   270

253–9: sterte] *jump*   That] *as if*   quake] *tremble*   o-lofte] *aloft*
260–6: rewen] *pity*   fantasie] *imagining*   drye] *suffer*   aspre] *bitter*
267–70: languor] *listlessness*   pyne] *suffering*   redere] *reader*   devyne] *imagine*

That swich a wo my wit kan nat diffyne.
On ydel for to wryte it sholde I swynke,
Whan that my wit is wery it to thinke.

The first half of Book 5 is taken up with Troilus and Pandarus' fruit-
less waiting for Criseyde's return, killing the time. They stay with the
generous Sarpedon, and return home with Troilus in high hopes but
Pandarus dubious.

Thus Pandarus, with alle peyne and wo,
Made hym to dwelle; and at the wikes ende
Of Sarpedoun they toke hir leve tho,   500
And on hire wey they spedden hem to wende.
Quod Troilus, 'Now Lord me grace sende,
That I may fynden at myn hom-comynge
Criseyde comen!' And therwith gan he singe.

'Ye, haselwode!' thoughte this Pandare,   505
And to hymself ful softeliche he seyde,
'God woot, refreyden may this hote fare,

271–3: diffyne] *describe*   it to thinke] *even to think about it*
498–504: peyne] *pains*   wikes] *week's*   comen] *arrived*
505–7: haselwode] *fat chance! (expression of scepticism)*   refreyden] *freeze
over*   hote fare] *hot passion*

97

Er Calkas sende Troilus Criseyde!'
But natheles, he japed thus, and pleyde,
And swor, ywys, his herte hym wel bihighte   510
She wolde come as sone as ever she myghte.

Whan they unto the paleys were ycomen
Of Troilus, they doun of hors alighte,
And to the chambre hire wey than han they nomen;
And into tyme that it gan to nyghte   515
They spaken of Criseyde the brighte.
And after this, whan that hem bothe leste,
They spedde hem fro the soper unto reste.

On morwe, as soone as day bygan to clere,
This Troilus gan of his sleep t'abrayde,   520
And to Pandare, his owen brother deere,
'For love of God,' ful pitously he sayde,
'As go we sen the palais of Criseyde;
For syn we yet may have namore feste,
So lat us sen hir paleys atte leeste.'   525

508–11: pleyde] *played along*   bihighte] *told*
512–18: nomen] *took*   into tyme] *until the time*   nyghte] *become night*
519–25: abrayde] *wake up*   atte leeste] *at least*

And therwithal, his meyne for to blende,
A cause he fond in towne for to go,
And to Criseydes hous they gonnen wende.
But Lord, this sely Troilus was wo!
Hym thoughte his sorwful herte braste a-two.   530
For whan he saugh hire dores spered alle,
Wel neigh for sorwe adoun he gan to falle.

Therwith, whan he was war and gan biholde
How shet was every wyndow of the place,
As frost, hym thoughte, his herte gan to colde;   535
For which with chaunged deedlich pale face,
Withouten word, he forthby gan to pace;
And as God wolde, he gan so faste ride,
That no wight of his contenance espide.

Than seide he thus: 'O paleys desolat,   540
O hous of houses whilom best ihight,
O paleys empty and disconsolat,
O thow lanterne of which queynt is the light,

526-32: meyne] *household*   blende] *deceive (blind)*   sely] *hapless*   braste]
would break   spered] *barred*
533-9: shet] *shut up*   forthby] *past*   ride] *ride away*
540-3: ihight] *regarded*   queynt] *quenched*

O paleys, whilom day, that now art night,
Wel oughtestow to falle, and I to dye,   545
Syn she is went that wont was us to gye!

'O paleis, whilom crowne of houses alle,
Enlumyned with sonne of alle blisse!
O ryng, fro which the ruby is out falle,
O cause of wo, that cause hast been of lisse!   550
Yet, syn I may no bet, fayn wolde I kisse
Thy colde dores, dorste I for this route;
And farwel shryne, of which the seynt is oute!'

Therwith he caste on Pandarus his ye,
With chaunged face, and pitous to biholde;   555
And whan he myghte his tyme aright aspie,
Ay as he rood to Pandarus he tolde
His newe sorwe and ek his joies olde,
So pitously and with so ded an hewe
That every wight myghte on his sorwe rewe.   560

544–6: whilom] *at one time*   gye] *lead*
547–53: Enlumyned] *illuminated*   lisse] *joy*   dorste I] *if I dared*   route]
crowd
554–60: tyme] *opportunity*   Ay] *all the time*   so ded an hewe] *so deathly a*
colour   rewe] *take pity*

Fro thennesforth he rideth up and down,
And every thyng com him to remembraunce
As he rood forby places of the town
In which he whilom hadde al his plesaunce.
'Lo, yonder saugh ich last my lady daunce;   565
And in that temple, with hir eyen cleere,
Me kaughte first my righte lady dere . . .'

Meanwhile Criseyde is 'upon that other side . . . with women fewe,
among the Grekis stronge' (687–8), in deep distress but determined
to return to Troy. But then Diomede makes his play for her, when she
is at her most vulnerable.

This Diomede, of whom yow telle I gan,
Goth now withinne hymself ay arguynge
With al the sleghte and al that evere he kan,
How he may best, with shortest taryinge,
Into his net Criseydes herte brynge.   775
To this entent he koude nevere fyne;
To fisshen hire he leyde out hook and lyne.

561–7: forby] *past*   whilom] *in past times*   kaughte] *caught sight of*
771–7: gan] *started*   sleghte] *ingenuity*   kan] *knows how to act*   taryinge]
delay   To this entent] *from this objective*   fyne] *stop*

101

But natheles, wel in his herte he thoughte
That she nas nat withoute a love in Troie,
For nevere sythen he hire thennes broughte   780
Ne koude he sen hire laughe or make joie.
He nyst how best hire herte for t'acoye.
'But for t'asay,' he seyde, 'naught n'agreveth;
For he that naught n'assaieth naught n'acheveth.'

Yet seyde he to hymself upon a nyght,   785
'Now am I not a fool, that woot wel how
Hire wo for love is of another wight,
And hereupon to gon assaye hire now?
I may wel wite it nyl nat ben my prow,
For wise folk in bookes it expresse: 790
"Men shal not wowe a wight in hevynesse."

'But whoso myghte wynnen swich a flour
From hym for whom she morneth nyght and day,
He myghte seyn he were a conquerour.'
And right anon, as he that bold was ay,   795

778–84: Ne koude he] *had he*   nyst] *didn't know*   acoye] *soothe*   asay] *try*
n'agreveth] *does no harm*   assaieth] *makes an attempt*
785–91: woot] *know*   wo for love] *love misery*   hereupon] *now*   assaye]
approach   prow] *benefit*   "Men ... hevynesse"] *'you mustn't woo somebody
when they are sad'*
792–5: whoso] *someone who*   morneth] *longs for*   seyn] *claim*   bold]
adventurous   ay] *always*

Thoughte in his herte, 'Happe how happe may,
Al sholde I dye, I wol hire herte seche.
I shal namore lesen but my speche.'

This Diomede, as bokes us declare,
Was in his nedes prest and courageous,   800
With sterne vois and myghty lymes square,
Hardy, testif, strong, and chivalrous
Of dedes, lik his fader Tideus.
And som men seyn he was of tonge large;
And heir he was of Calydoigne and Arge.   805

Criseyde mene was of hire stature;
Therto of shap, of face, and ek of cheere,
Ther myghte ben no fairer creature.
And ofte tymes this was hire manere:
To gon ytressed with hire heres clere   810
Doun by hire coler at hire bak byhynde,
Which with a thred of gold she wolde bynde;

796–8: Happe how happe may] *whatever happens*   Al] *even though*   seche] *ask for*   lessen] *lose*   speche] *words*
799–805: nedes] *ambitions*   prest] *impulsive*   lymes square] *stolid limbs*   testif] *impetuous*   of tonge large] *boastful (or physically large-tongued?)*
Calydoigne] *Calydon in Asia Minor, ruled over by Oeneus, Diomede's grandfather*   Arge] *Argos*
806–12: mene] *average*   cheere] *manner*   manere] *way of dressing*   clere] *shining*   coler] *collar*

And, save hire browes joyneden yfeere,
Ther nas no lak, in aught I kan espien.
But for to speken of hire eyen cleere, 815
Lo, trewely, they writen that hire syen
That Paradys stood formed in hire yen.
And with hire riche beaute evere more
Strof love in hire ay, which of hem was more.

She sobre was, ek symple, and wys withal, 820
The best ynorisshed ek that myghte be,
And goodly of hire speche in general,
Charitable, estatlich, lusty, fre;
Ne nevere mo ne lakked hire pite;
Tendre-herted, slydynge of corage; 825
But trewely, I kan nat telle hire age.

And Troilus wel woxen was in highte,
And complet formed by proporcioun
So wel that kynde it nought amenden myghte;
Yong, fressh, strong, and hardy as lyoun; 830

813–19: save] *except that*   joyneden yfeere] *joined together (she was a monobrow)*
espien] *see*   syen] *saw*   Strof love] *love competed*
820–6: symple] *unaffected*   ynorisshed] *brought up*   estatlich] *dignified*   lusty]
healthy   fre] *noble*   pite] *sympathy*   slydynge] *variable*   corage] *mood*
827–30: woxen] *developed*   complet] *perfectly*   kynde] *Nature*   hardy]
vigorous

Trewe as stiel in ech condicioun;
Oon of the beste entecched creature,
That is or shal whil that the world may dure.

And certeynly in storye it is yfounde,
That Troilus was nevere unto no wight,   835
As in his tyme, in no degree secounde
In durring don that longeth to a knyght.
Al myghte a geant passen hym of myght,
His herte ay with the first and with the beste
Stood paregal, to durre don that him leste.   840

But for to tellen forth of Diomede:
It fel that after, on the tenthe day
Syn that Criseyde out of the citee yede,
This Diomede, as fressh as braunche in May,
Com to the tente ther as Calkas lay,   845
And feyned him with Calkas han to doone;
But what he mente, I shal yow tellen sone.

831–3: stiel] *steel*   condicioun] *quality*   entecched] *endowed*   dure] *last*
834–40: secounde] *second best*   durring don] *daring in action*   longeth to] *is
proper to*   Al] *even if*   geant] *giant*   myght] *strength*   paregal] *equal*   durre
don] *dare to do*
841–7: to tellen forth] *getting back to*   fel] *happened*   yede] *went*   fressh] *lively*
feyned] *pretended*   han to doone] *had business with*   mente] *intended*

Criseyde, at shorte wordes for to telle,
Welcomed hym and doun hym by hire sette:
And he was ethe ynough to maken dwelle!   850
And after this, withouten longe lette,
The spices and the wyn men forth hem fette;
And forth they speke of this and that yfeere,
As frendes doon, of which som shal ye heere.

He gan first fallen of the werre in speche   855
Bitwixe hem and the folk of Troie town;
And of th'assege he gan hire ek biseche
To telle hym what was hire opynyoun;
Fro that demaunde he so descendeth down
To axen hire if that hire straunge thoughte   860
The Grekis gise and werkes that they wrought,

And whi hire fader tarieth so longe
To wedden hire unto som worthy wight?
Criseyde, that was in hire peynes stronge
For love of Troilus, hire owen knyght,   865

848–54: ethe] *easy*   lette] *delay*   yfeere] *together*
855–61: fallen] *turn to*   assege] *siege*   descendeth down] *went on to*   gise]
manner   werkes] *things*
862–5: tarieth] *is delaying*   in hire peynes stronge] *suffering badly*

As ferforth as she konnyng hadde or myght
Answerde hym tho; but as of his entente,
It semed nat she wiste what he mente.

But natheles, this ilke Diomede
Gan in hymself assure, and thus he seyde: 870
'If ich aright have taken of yow hede,
Me thynketh thus, O lady myn, Criseyde,
That syn I first hond on your bridel leyde
Whan ye out come of Troie by the morwe,
Ne koude I nevere sen yow but in sorwe.   875

'Kan I nat seyn what may the cause be,
But if for love of som Troian it were,
The which right sore wolde athynken me
That ye for any wight that dwelleth there
Sholden spille a quarter of a tere   880
Or pitously youreselven so bigile,
For dredelees, it is nought worth the whyle.

866–8: As ferforth as] *as far as*   konnyng] *understanding*
869–75: assure] *grow confident*   hede] *observation*   bridel] *her horse's bridle*
by the morwe] *in the morning*   koude I] *have I*
876–82: athynken] *displease*   bigile] *mislead*   dredelees] *doubtless*

'The folk of Troie, as who seyth, alle and some
In prisoun ben, as ye youreselven se;
Nor thennes shal not oon on-lyve come   885
For al the gold atwixen sonne and see.
Trusteth wel, and understondeth me.
Ther shal not oon to mercy gon on-lyve,
Al were he lord of worldes twies fyve!

'Swich wreche on hem for fecchyng of Eleyne   890
Ther shal ben take, er that we hennes wende,
That Manes, which that goddes ben of peyne,
Shal ben agast that Grekes wol hem shende,
And men shul drede, unto the worldes ende,
From hennesforth to ravysshen any queene,   895
So cruel shal oure wreche on hem be seene.'

We reach the date by which Criseyde has promised to return, but she
stays in the Greek camp.

The brighte Venus folwede and ay taughte
The wey ther brode Phebus doun alighte;

883–9: as who seyth] *as you might say*
890–6: wreche] *vengeance*   fecchyng] *taking*   Manes] *the Shades – gods of the
underworld*   agast] *fearful*   shende] *destroy*   drede] *be afraid to*   ravysshen]
carry off
1016–17: Venus] *the evening star*   taught / The wey ther] *showed the path where*
brode Phebus] *the Sun (looking wide as it sets)*

108

And Cynthea hir char-hors overraughte
To whirle out of the Lyon, if she myghte;
And Signifer his candels sheweth brighte   1020
Whan that Criseyde unto hire bedde wente
Inwith hire fadres faire brighte tente,

Retorning in hire soule ay up and down
The wordes of this sodeyn Diomede,
His grete estat, and perel of the town,   1025
And that she was allone and hadde nede
Of frendes help; and thus bygan to brede
The cause why, the sothe for to telle,
That she took fully purpos for to dwelle.

The morwen com, and gostly for to speke,   1030
This Diomede is come unto Criseyde,
And shortly, lest that ye my tale breke,
So wel he for hymselven spak and seyde,
That alle hir sikes soore adown he leyde;

1018–22: Cynthea] *the Moon*   char-hors] *chariot-horse*   overraughte] *urged*
extremely   the Lyon] *the constellation Leo*   Signifer] *the Zodiac*   candels]
bright stars
1023–9: Retorning] *going over*   soule] *mind*   sodeyn] *impulsive*   estat] *social
position*   perel] *peril*   brede] *take root*   took fully purpos] *decided definitely*
1030–4: morwen] *morning*   gostly] *truly*   breke] *interrupt*   sikes soore]
heartfelt sighs   leyde] *allayed*

And finaly, the sothe for to seyne,   1035
He refte hire of the grete of al hire peyne.

And after this the storie telleth us,
That she hym yaf the faire baye stede
The which he ones wan of Troilus;
And ek a broche (and that was litel nede)   1040
That Troilus was, she yaf this Diomede.
And ek, the bet from sorwe hym to releve,
She made him were a pencel of hire sleve.

I fynde ek in stories elleswhere,
Whan thorugh the body hurt was Diomede   1045
Of Troilus, tho wep she many a teere
Whan that she saugh his wyde wowndes blede,
And that she took, to kepen hym, good hede;
And for to hele him of his sorwes smerte
Men seyn – I not – that she yaf hym hire herte.   1050

But trewely, the storie telleth us,

1035–6: refte] *relieved*   grete] *greatest*
1037–43: yaf] *gave*   baye] *bay*   wan of] *won from*   ek] *also*   Troilus]
Troilus'   releve] *reassure*   a pencel of] *as a pennant*
1044–50: Of Troilus] *by Troilus*   kepen] *look after*   I not] *I don't know*

Ther made nevere womman moore wo
Than she, whan that she falsed Troilus.
She seyde, 'Allas! For now is clene ago
My name of trouthe in love for everemo!   1055
For I have falsed oon, the gentileste
That ever was, and oon the worthieste!

'Allas, of me, unto the worldes ende,
Shal neyther ben ywriten nor ysonge
No good word, for thise bokes wol me shende.   1060
O, rolled shal I ben on many a tonge!
Thorughout the world my belle shal be ronge!
And wommen moost wol haten me of alle.
Allas, that swich a cas me sholde falle!

'They wol seyn, in as muche as in me is,   1065
I have hem don deshonour, weylaway!
Al be I nat the first that dide amys,
What helpeth that to don my blame awey?
But syn I se ther is no bettre way,

1052-7: made ... wo] *was sorrowful*   falsed] *proved false to*   ago] *gone*
1058-64: ysonge] *sung*   shende] *destroy*   rolled] *turned over in the mind*   my
belle shal be ronge] *my story shall be told (perhaps the phrase that suggested to
Chaucer's successor Henryson the affliction of leprosy he visited on her in* The
Testament of Cresseid)   moost ... of alle] *especially*   cas] *fate*
1065-9: in as muche as in me is] *in so far as it is my fault*   weylaway!] *alas!*

And that to late is now for me to rewe,   1070
To Diomede algate I wol be trewe.

'But Troilus, syn I no bettre may,
And syn that thus departen ye and I,
Yet preye I God, so yeve yow right good day,
As for the gentileste, trewely,   1075
That evere I say, to serven feythfully,
And best kan ay his lady honour kepe:'
And with that word she brast anon to wepe.

Troilus dreams of Criseyde making love to a violent boar, interpreted
correctly (but without credit) by Cassandra, Troilus' sister, as a figure
of Diomede whose grandfather Meleager fought with a boar. Troilus
does not believe her until he sees a brooch that he gave Criseyde on a
cloak that Deiphebus won in battle from Diomede. After a final ex-
change of letters, Fate drives to its conclusion: there is no help for it.

Gret was the sorwe and pleynte of Troilus;
But forth hire cours Fortune ay gan to holde.   1745
Criseyde loveth the sone of Tideus,

1070–1: rewe] *regret it*   algate] *at least*
1072–8: no bettre] *any more*   departen] *part*   yeve] *give*   good day]
greeting   As for] *as*   gentileste] *most noble*   say] *saw*   brast] *burst*
1744–6: pleynte] *lamenting*   holde] *pursue*   the sone of Tideus] *Diomede*

And Troilus moot wepe in cares colde.
Swich is this world, who-so it can biholde:
In ech estat is litel hertes reste.
God leve us for to take it for the beste!   1750

In many cruel bataille, out of drede,
Of Troilus, this ilke noble knyght,
As men may in thise olde bokes rede,
Was seen his knyghthod and his grete myght.
And dredeles, his ire, day and nyght,   1755
Ful cruwely the Grekis ay aboughte;
And alwey most this Diomede he soughte.

And ofte tyme, I fynde that they mette
With blody strokes and with wordes grete,
Assayinge how hire speres weren whette;   1760
And God it woot, with many a cruel hete
Gan Troilus upon his helm to bete!
But natheles, Fortune it naught ne wolde
Of oothers hond that either deyen sholde.

1747–50: moot] *must*   estat] *case*   leve] *grant*
1751–7: out of drede] *without doubt*   ilke] *same*   dredeles] *doubtless*
aboughte] *paid for*
1758–64: mette] *encountered each other*   Assayinge] *testing*   whette] *sharpened*
woot] *knows*   hete] *fervour*   helm] *helmet*

And if I hadde ytaken for to write   1765
The armes of this ilke worthi man,
Than wolde I of his batailles endite.
But for that I to writen first bigan
Of his love, I have seyd as I kan.
His worthi dedes, whoso list hem heere,   1770
Reed Dares, he kan telle hem alle ifeere –

Bysechyng every lady bright of hewe,
And every gentil womman, what she be,
That al be that Criseyde was untrewe,
That for that gilt she be nat wroth with me.   1775
Ye may hire gilt in other bokes se;
And gladlier I wol write, if yow leste,
Penolopees trouthe and good Alceste.

N'y sey nat this al oonly for thise men,
But moost for wommen that bitraised be   1780
Thorugh false folk – God yeve hem sorwe, amen! –
That with hire grete wit and subtilte

1765–71: ytaken] *undertaken*   endite] *write*   Dares] *Dares the Phrygian,
supposed author of an account of the Trojan War, written before Homer and
translated into Latin in the fifth century AD: one of a series of spurious
predecessors invoked by Chaucer*   ifeere] *together*
1772–8: what] *whatever*   wroth] *angry*   gladlier] *more willingly*   leste]
wanted   Penolopees ... Alceste] *(Penelope and Alcestis, both exemplarily
faithful wives)*
1779–82: bitraised] *betrayed*   subtilte] *ingenuity*

Bitraise yow. And this commeveth me
To speke, and in effect yow alle I preye,
Beth war of men, and herkeneth what I seye!   1785

Go, litel bok, go litel myn tragedye,
Ther God thi makere yet, er that he dye,
So sende myght to make in som comedye!
But litel book, no makyng thou n'envie,
But subgit be to alle poesye;   1790
And kis the steppes where as thow seest pace
Virgile, Ovide, Omer, Lucan, and Stace.

In a rather uncomfortable coda – not always admired by the poem's
readers – borrowed from the experience of Arcite in Boccaccio's
Teseida (the source of Chaucer's *Knight's Tale*), Troilus is taken up
after his death into the eighth sphere for judgement and an eternal
place 'Ther as Mercurye sorted hym to dwelle' (1827). And we are
urged to return to the more trustworthy Christian world, the world
in which God 'which that right for love / Upon a crois (cross), oure
soules for to beye (redeem), / First starf (died), and roos, and sit in
hevene above.'

1783–5: commeveth] *prompts*
1786–92: Ther God] *may God*   thi makere] *your author*   make in] *write in*
poetry   n'envie] *go in competition with*   subgit] *reverential*   Omer, Lucan,
and Stace *Homer, Lucan (author of the* Pharsalia*) and Statius (author of the*
Thebaid, *much drawn on in* Troilus*).*

Chaucers Wordes Unto Adam, His Owne Scriveyn

∽

At the start of the coda to *Troilus* Chaucer ambitiously commends his 'litel bok, litel myn tragedye' to the company of the great poets – 'Virgile, Ovide, Omer, Lucan, and Stace', but pleads that, given that 'ther is so gret diversite / In Englissh and in writing of oure tonge', no one will 'myswrite' or 'mysmetre' it 'for defaute of tonge' (language). He expresses the same misgivings in this short poem addressed to his scribe Adam:

> Adam scriveyn, if ever it thee bifalle
> Boece or Troylus for to wryten newe,
> Under thy long lokkes, thou most have the scale

1–3: scriveyn] *scribe*   Boece] *Chaucer's translation of Boethius*   wryten newe] *copy again*   scale] *a skin disease*

But after my making thow wryte more trewe;
So ofte adaye I mot thy werk renewe,   5
It to correcte and eke to rubbe and scrape,
And al is thorugh thy neglicence and rape.

4–7: making] *writing*   trewe] *accurately*   renewe] *correct*   rubbe]
erase   scrape] *scrape off*   rape] *haste*

The Legend of Good Women

∾

With this long poem, perhaps based on Boccaccio's book *Of Famous Women* (corresponding to another book of Boccaccio's *Of Famous Men* and, perhaps more significantly, echoing Ovid's *Heroides*), Chaucer returns to the dream vision of the major works before *Troilus*. In its elaborate and beautiful prologue – in the nineteenth century the most loved piece of Chaucer apart from the *General Prologue* to *The Canterbury Tales* – we are told that Chaucer is composing this work at the request of the goddess-queen Alceste to atone for having written ill of women in his representation of the faithless Criseyde. There are two versions of the prologue,

called F and G; the prevailing modern view is that F, which is the one
I have drawn on here, is both earlier and better (G only survives in
one manuscript).

A thousand tymes have I herd men telle
That ther ys joy in hevene and peyne in helle,
And I acorde wel that it ys so;
But, natheles, yet wot I wel also
That ther nis noon dwellyng in this contree
That eyther hath in hevene or helle ybe,
Ne may of hit noon other weyes witen
But as he hath herd seyd or founde it writen;
For by assay ther may no man it preve.
But God forbede but men shulde leve   10
Wel more thing than men han seen with ye!
Men shal not wenen every thing a lye
But yf himself yt seeth or elles dooth.
For, God wot, thing is never the lasse sooth,
Thogh every wight ne may it nat ysee.
Bernard the monk ne saugh nat all, pardee!

1–10: acorde] *agree*   wot I] *I know*   assay] *testing*   but men shulde] *that men
should not*
11–16: ye] *their eyes*   wenen] *think*   sooth] *true*

Than mote we to bokes that we fynde,
Thurgh whiche that olde thinges ben in mynde,
And to the doctrine of these olde wyse,
Yeve credence, in every skylful wise,   20
That tellen of these olde appreved stories
Of holynesse, of regnes, of victories,
Of love, of hate, of other sondry thynges,
Of whiche I may not maken rehersynges.
And yf that olde bokes were aweye,
Yloren were of remembraunce the keye.
Wel ought us thanne honouren and beleve
These bokes, there we han noon other preve.
And as for me, though that I konne but lyte,
On bokes for to rede I me delyte,   30
And to hem yive I feyth and ful credence,
And in myn herte have hem in reverence
So hertely, that ther is game noon
That fro my bokes maketh me to goon,
But yt be seldom on the holyday,
Save, certeynly, whan that the month of May

17–20: mote we] *we must turn to*   skylful] *technical*
21–30: appreved] *proved true*   regnes] *reigns*   rehersynges] *reference*   aweye]
missing   Yloren] *lost*   there] *wherever*
31–6: yive I] *I give*   hertely] *devotedly*   holyday] *Church holiday*

Is comen, and that I here the foules synge,
And that the floures gynnen for to sprynge,
Farewel my bok and my devocioun!
Now have I thanne ek this condicioun,   40
That, of al the floures in the mede,
Thanne love I most thise floures white and rede,
Swiche as men callen daysyes in our toun.
To hem have I so gret affeccioun,
As I seyde erst, whanne comen is the May,
That in my bed ther daweth me no day
That I nam up and walkyng in the mede
To seen this flour ayein the sonne sprede,
Whan it upryseth erly by the morwe.
That blisful sighte softneth al my sorwe,   50
So glad am I, whan that I have presence
Of it, to doon it alle reverence,
As she that is of alle floures flour,
Fulfilled of al vertu and honour,
And evere ilyke faire and fressh of hewe;

37–40: devocioun] *attention*   condicioun] *tendency*
41–50: mede] *meadow*   erst] *already*   daweth me] *dawns for me*   sprede] *open*
51–5: evere ilyke] *unfailingly*

And I love it, and ever ylike newe,
And evere shal, til that myn herte dye.
Al swere I nat, of this I wol nat lye;
Ther loved no wight hotter in his lyve.
And whan that hit ys eve, I renne blyve,   60
As sone as evere the sonne gynneth weste,
To seen this flour, how it wol go to reste
For fere of nyght, so hateth she derknesse.
Hire chere is pleynly sprad in the brightnesse
Of the sonne, for ther yt wol unclose.
Allas, that I ne had Englyssh, ryme or prose,
Suffisant this flour to preyse aryght!
But helpeth, ye that han konnyng and myght,
Ye lovers that kan make of sentement;
In this cas oghte ye be diligent   70
To forthren me somwhat in my labour,
Whethir ye ben with the leef or with the flour.
For wel I wot that ye han her-biforn
Of makyng ropen, and lad awey the corn,
And I come after, glenyng here and there,

56–60: newe] *repeatedly*   Al swere I nat] *I am not prevaricating*   blyve] *quickly*
61–70: weste] *go westward*   chere] *display*   kan make of] *can write poetry about*
71–5: forthren] *advance*   Of makyng ropen] *reaped poetry*

And am ful glad yf I may fynde an ere
Of any goodly word that ye han left.
And thogh it happen me rehercen eft
That ye han in your fresshe songes sayd,
Forbereth me, and beth nat evele apayd,   80
Syn that ye see I do yt in the honour
Of love, and eke in service of the flour
Whom that I serve as I have wit or myght.
She is the clernesse and the verray lyght
That in this derke world me wynt and ledeth.
The hert in-with my sorwfull brest yow dredeth
And loveth so sore that ye ben verrayly
The maistresse of my wit, and nothing I.
My word, my werk ys knyt so in youre bond
That, as an harpe obeieth to the hond   90
And maketh it soune after his fyngerynge,
Ryght so mowe ye oute of myn herte bringe
Swich vois, ryght as yow lyst, to laughe or pleyne.
Be ye my gide and lady sovereyne!
As to myn erthly god to yow I calle,

76–80: ere] *corn-ear*   rehercen] *repeat*   Forbereth] *bear with*   apayd] *repaid*
81–90: wynt] *winds (i.e. directs)*   nothing I] *I not at all*   knyt] *bound*
91–5: mowe] *can*   lyst] *want*   As to] *As*

124

Bothe in this werk and in my sorwes alle.
But wherfore that I spak, to yive credence
To olde stories and doon hem reverence,
And that men mosten more thyng beleve
Then men may seen at eye, or elles preve –   100
That shal I seyn, whanne that I see my tyme;
I may not al at-ones speke in ryme.
My besy gost, that thursteth alwey newe
To seen this flour so yong, so fressh of hewe,
Constreyned me with so gledy desir
That in myn herte I feele yet the fir
That made me to ryse er yt were day –
And this was now the firste morwe of May –
With dredful hert and glad devocioun,
For to ben at the resureccioun   110
Of this flour, whan that yt shulde unclose
Agayn the sonne, that roos as red as rose,
That in the brest was of the beste, that day,
That Agenores doghtre ladde away.
And doun on knes anoon-ryght I me sette,

96–100: preve] *prove by experiment*
101–10: tyme] *opportunity*   gost] *spirit*   gledy] *burning*   dredful] *fearful*
resureccioun] *rising*
111–15: unclose] *open out*   beste] *the Bull constellation*   Agenores doghtre]
Europa

And, as I koude, this fresshe flour I grette,
Knelyng alwey, til it unclosed was,
Upon the smale, softe, swote gras,
That was with floures swote enbrouded al,
Of swich swetnesse and swich odour overal,   120
That, for to speke of gomme, or herbe, or tree,
Comparisoun may noon ymaked bee;
For yt surmounteth pleynly alle odoures,
And of riche beaute alle floures.
Forgeten hadde the erthe his pore estat
Of wynter, that hym naked made and mat,
And with his swerd of cold so sore greved;
Now hath th' atempre sonne all that releved,
That naked was, and clad him new agayn.
The smale foules, of the sesoun fayn,   130
That from the panter and the net ben scaped,
Upon the foweler, that hem made awhaped
In wynter, and distroyed hadde hire brood,
In his dispit hem thoghte yt did hem good
To synge of hym, and in hir song despise

116–20: enbrouded] *embroidered*
121–30: gomme] *gum*   mat] *defeated*   atempre] *temperate*   fayn] *rejoicing*
131–5: panter] *snare*   awhaped] *confounded*   brood] *nestlings*

The foule cherl that, for his coveytise,
Had hem betrayed with his sophistrye.
This was hire song: 'The foweler we deffye,
And al his craft.' And somme songen clere
Layes of love, that joye it was to here,   140
In worship and in preysinge of hir make;
And for the newe blisful somers sake,
Upon the braunches ful of blosmes softe,
In hire delyt they turned hem ful ofte,
And songen, 'Blessed be Seynt Valentyn,
For on his day I chees yow to be myn,
Withouten repentyng, myn herte swete!'
And therwithalle hire bekes gonnen meete,
Yeldyng honour and humble obeysaunces
To love, and diden hire other observaunces   150
That longeth onto love and to nature;
Construeth that as yow lyst, I do no cure.
And thoo that hadde doon unkyndenesse –
As dooth the tydif, for newfangelnesse –
Besoghte mercy of hir trespassynge,

136–40: sophistrye] *trickery*
141–50: make] *mate*   repentyng] *reservation*   bekes] *beaks*   Yeldyng] *offering*
151–5: longeth] *pertain*   Construeth] *Judge*   cure] *care*   thoo] *those*   tydif]
small bird associated with infidelity   newfangelnesse] *love of change*

And humblely songen hire repentynge,
And sworen on the blosmes to be trewe
So that hire makes wolde upon hem rewe,
And at the laste maden hire acord.
Al founde they Daunger for a tyme a lord,   160
Yet Pitee, thurgh his stronge gentil myght,
Forgaf, and made Mercy passen Ryght,
Thurgh innocence and ruled Curtesye.
But I ne clepe nat innocence folye,
Ne fals pitee, for vertu is the mene,
As Etik seith; in swich maner I mene.
And thus thise foweles, voide of al malice,
Acordeden to love, and laften vice
Of hate, and songen alle of oon acord,
'Welcome, somer, oure governour and lord!'   170
And Zepherus and Flora gentilly
Yaf to the floures, softe and tenderly,
Hire swoote breth, and made hem for to sprede,
As god and goddesse of the floury mede;
In which me thoghte I myghte, day by day,

156–60: rewe] *take pity*   Daunger] *disapproval in love*
161–70: passen] *surpass*   Ryght] *justice*   Curtesye] *abiding by the rules of
love*   mene] *balance*
171–5: Zepherus] *the West Wind*   Flora] *goddess of flowers*   Yaf] *gave*   sprede]
open out

Duellen alwey, the joly month of May,
Withouten slep, withouten mete or drynke.
Adoun ful softely I gan to synke,
And, lenynge on myn elbowe and my syde,
The longe day I shoop me for t'abide   180
For nothing elles, and I shal nat lye,
But for to loke upon the dayesie,
That wel by reson men it calle may
The 'dayesye,' or elles the 'ye of day,'
The emperice and flour of floures alle.
I pray to God that faire mote she falle,
And alle that loven floures, for hire sake!
But natheles, ne wene nat that I make
In preysing of the flour agayn the leef,
No more than of the corn agayn the sheef;   190
For, as to me, nys lever noon ne lother.
I nam withholden yit with never nother;
Ne I not who serveth leef ne who the flour.
Wel browken they her service or labour;
For this thing is al of another tonne,

176–80: shoop] *prepared*
181–90: ye] *eye*   falle] *prosper*   agayn] *against*
191–5: lever] *preferable*   lother] *less favoured*   withholden] *committed to*   with
never nother] *to either party*   I not] *I don't know*   browken] *may they gain*
(brook)   of another tonne] *of a different vintage)*

Of olde storye, er swich stryf was begonne.
Whan that the sonne out of the south gan weste,
And that this flour gan close and goon to reste
For derknesse of the nyght, the which she dredde,
Hom to myn hous ful swiftly I me spedde   200
To goon to reste, and erly for to ryse,
To seen this flour to sprede, as I devyse.
And in a litel herber that I have,
That benched was on turves fressh ygrave,
I bad men sholde me my couche make;
For deyntee of the newe someres sake,
I bad hem strawen floures on my bed.
Whan I was leyd and had myn eyen hed,
I fel on slepe within an houre or twoo.
Me mette how I lay in the medewe thoo,   210
To seen this flour that I so love and drede;
And from afer com walkyng in the mede
The god of Love, and in his hand a quene,
And she was clad in real habit grene.
A fret of gold she hadde next her heer,

201–10: devyse] *describe*   herber] *garden-corner*   benched] *founded*   turves]
lawn-grass   ygrave] *dug*   hed] *shaded*   mette] *dreamed*   thoo] *then*
211–15: drede] *venerate*   real] *royal*   fret] *ornament*

And upon that a whit corowne she beer
With flourouns smale, and I shal nat lye;
For al the world, ryght as a dayesye
Ycorouned ys with white leves lyte,
So were the flowrouns of hire coroune white.   220
For of o perle fyn, oriental,
Hire white coroune was ymaked al;
For which the white coroune above the grene
Made hire lyk a daysie for to sene,
Considered eke hir fret of gold above.
Yclothed was this myghty god of Love
In silk, enbrouded ful of grene greves,
In-with a fret of rede rose-leves,
The fresshest syn the world was first bygonne.
His gilte heer was corowned with a sonne   230
Instede of gold, for hevynesse and wyghte.
Therwith me thoghte his face shoon so bryghte
That wel unnethes myghte I him beholde;
And in his hand me thoghte I saugh him holde
Twoo firy dartes as the gledes rede,

216–20: flourouns] *little flowers*
221–30: o] *one, the same*   Considered] *considering*   greves] *sprays*
231–5: wyghte] *weight*   unnethes] *hardly*   gledes] *coals*

And aungelyke hys wynges saugh I sprede.
And al be that men seyn that blynd ys he,
Algate me thoghte that he myghte se;
For sternely on me he gan byholde,
So that his loking dooth myn herte colde.   240
And by the hand he held this noble quene
Corowned with whit and clothed al in grene,
So womanly, so benigne, and so meke,
That in this world, thogh that men wolde seke,
Half hire beaute shulde men nat fynde
In creature that formed ys by kynde.
And therfore may I seyn, as thynketh me,
This song in preysyng of this lady fre:

Balade

Hyd, Absolon, thy gilte tresses clere;
Ester, ley thou thy meknesse al adown;   250
Hyd, Jonathas, al thy frendly manere;
Penalopee and Marcia Catoun,

236–40: al be that] *although*   Algate] *nevertheless*
241–50: kynde] *Nature*   fre] *noble*
251–2: Absolon] *Absolom, the beautiful son of David*   gilte] *golden*   Ester
Esther, a Biblical model of humility   Jonathas] *Jonathan, David's companion*
Penalopee and Marcia Catoun] *Penelope and Marcia, faithful classical wives of
Odysseus and Cato the Younger respectively*

132

Make of youre wifhod no comparysoun;
Hyde ye youre beautes, Ysoude and Eleyne:
My lady cometh, that al this may disteyne.

Thy faire body, lat yt nat appere,
Lavyne; and thou, Lucresse of Rome toun,
And Polixene, that boghten love so dere,
And Cleopatre, with al thy passyoun,
Hyde ye your trouthe of love and your renoun;   260
And thou, Tisbe, that hast for love swich peyne:
My lady cometh, that al this may disteyne.

Herro, Dido, Laudomia, alle yfere,
And Phillis, hangyng for thy Demophoun,
And Canace, espied by thy chere,
Ysiphile, betrayed with Jasoun,
Maketh of your trouthe neythir boost ne soun;
Nor Ypermystre or Adriane, ye tweyne:
My lady cometh, that al this may dysteyne.

&

253–60:   wifhod] wifely quality   Ysoude] Isolde   Eleyne] Helen   disteyne]
surpass   Lavyne] Lavinia, Aeneas' wife   Lucresse] Lucretia   Polixene]
Polyxena, Achilles's faithful lover
261–9: Tisbe] Thisbe, fated lover of Pyramus   Herro] *Hero*   Laudomia . . .]
Laodamia, Canace, etc. – all ill-fated women lovers from Ovid's Heroides

Truth

This elegant lyric in four stanzas of rhyme royal is the most popular of Chaucer's short poems, occurring in twenty-two manuscripts. Of the series of short poems on Boethian themes – transience and the influence of *Fortiune* – this poem, addressed in its concluding *envoy* to Richard II, has been speculatively dated to 1398–9 and so is interesting to read with Chaucer's 'Complaint to His Purse', the last item in this selection (pp. 243–5).

Balade de Bon Conseyl

Flee fro the prees, and dwelle with sothfastnesse;
Suffyce unto thy thing, though it be smal,
For hord hath hate, and climbing tikelnesse,
Prees hath envye, and wele blent overal.
Savour no more thanne thee bihove shal,
Reule wel thyself, that other folk canst rede,
And trouthe thee shal delivere, it is no drede.

Tempest thee noght al croked to redresse
In trust of hir that turneth as a bal;
Gret reste stant in litel besinesse.   10
Be war therfore to sporne ayeyns an al,
Stryve not, as doth the crokke with the wal.
Daunte thyself, that dauntest otheres dede,
And trouthe thee shal delivere, it is no drede.

1–7: Balade de Bon Conseyl] *Ballad of Good Counsel*   prees] *crowd (at court)*
sothfastnesse] *truth*   thing] *possessions*   hord] *hoarding of wealth*   tikelnesse]
instability   blent] *blinds*   rede] *advise*   drede] *doubt*
8–14: Tempest] *agitate*   croked] *wrong*   hir] *Fortune*   bal] *wheel*   sporne]
kick   al] *awl (sharp implement)*   crokke] *jar*   Daunte] *rule*   dede] *deeds*

That thee is sent, receyve in buxumnesse;
The wrastling for this world axeth a fal.
Her is non hoom, her nis but wildernesse:
Forth, pilgrim, forth! Forth, beste, out of thy stal!
Know thi contree, look up, thank God of al;
Hold the heye wey and lat thy gost thee lede,   20
And trouthe thee shal delivere, it is no drede.

Envoy

Therfore, thou Vache, leve thyn old wrechednesse;
Unto the world leve now to be thral.
Crye him mercy, that of his hy goodnesse
Made thee of noght, and in especial   25
Draw unto him, and pray in general
For thee, and ek for other, hevenlich mede;
And trouthe thee shal delivere, it is no drede.

৯

15–21: buxumnesse] *obedience*   wrastling] *competing*   the heye wey] *the straight road*
22–8: Envoy] *concluding letter*   Vache] *Vache: proper name?*   leve] *stop*
mede] *rewar*

Lak of Stedfastnesse

୶

Balade

Somtyme the world was so stedfast and stable
That mannes word was obligacioun,
And now it is so fals and deceivable
That word and deed, as in conclusioun,
Ben nothing lyk, for turned up-so-doun
Is al this world for mede and wilfulnesse,
That al is lost for lak of stedfastnesse.

1–7: obligacioun] *guarantee*   mede] *bribery*

What maketh this world to be so variable
But lust that folk have in dissensioun?
For among us now a man is holde unable,   10
But if he can by som collusioun
Don his neighbour wrong or oppressioun.
What causeth this but wilful wrecchednesse,
That al is lost for lak of stedfastnesse?

Trouthe is put doun, resoun is holden fable,
Vertu hath now no dominacioun;
Pitee exyled, no man is merciable.
Through covetyse is blent discrecioun.
The world hath mad a permutacioun
Fro right to wrong, fro trouthe to fikelnesse,   20
That al is lost for lak of stedfastnesse.

Lenvoy to King Richard
O prince, desyre to be honourable,
Cherish thy folk and hate extorcioun.

8–14: lust] *taste*   unable] *ineffective*   collusioun] *trickery*
15–21: fable] *falsehood*   blent] *blinded*   fikelnesse] *unreliability*

Suffre nothing that may be reprevable
To thyn estat don in thy regioun.
Shew forth thy swerd of castigacioun,
Dred God, do law, love trouthe and worthinesse,
And wed thy folk agein to stedfastnesse.

&

24–8: reprevable] *damaging*

Lenvoy de Chaucer a Scogan

❧

This wise poem of old age and writing is addressed to Chaucer's court friend Henry Scogan, who was a generation younger than Chaucer and so is represented here as expressing surprise that the 'olde Grisel' (greybeard) Chaucer is continuing to 'ryme and playe' in his old age.

> Tobroken been the statutz hye in hevene
> That creat were eternally to dure,
> Syth that I see the bryghte goddis sevene

1–3: Tobroken   *broken*   statutz] *laws*   creat] *made*   Syth that] *since* goddis sevene] *seven planets*

143

Mowe wepe and wayle, and passioun endure,
As may in erthe a mortal creature.
Allas, fro whennes may thys thing procede,
Of which errour I deye almost for drede?

By word eterne whilom was it shape
That fro the fyfte sercle, in no manere,
Ne myght a drope of teeres doun escape.   10
But now so wepith Venus in hir spere
That with hir teeres she wol drenche us here.
Allas! Scogan, this is for thyn offence;
Thow causest this diluge of pestilence.

Hastow not seyd, in blaspheme of the goddis,
Thurgh pride, or thrugh thy grete rekelnesse,
Swich thing as in the lawe of love forbode is,
That, for thy lady sawgh nat thy distresse,
Therfore thow yave hir up at Michelmesse?
Allas! Scogan, of olde folk ne yonge   20
Was never erst Scogan blamed for his tonge.

4–7: Mowe] *must*   errour] *confusion*
8–14: shape] *designed*   fyfte] *fifth, Venus*   spere] *sphere*   diluge] *deluge*
15–21: rekelnesse] *rashness*   sawgh] *appreciated*   Michelnesse] *29 September*

Thow drowe in skorn Cupide eke to record
Of thilke rebel word that thow hast spoken,
For which he wol no lenger be thy lord.
And, Scogan, though his bowe be nat broken,
He wol nat with his arwes been ywroken
On the, ne me, ne noon of oure figure;
We shul of him have neyther hurt ne cure.

Now certes, frend, I dreed of thyn unhap,
Lest for thy gilt the wreche of Love procede   30
On alle hem that ben hoor and rounde of shap,
That ben so lykly folk in love to spede.
Than shal we for oure labour have no mede;
But wel I wot, thow wolt answere and saye,
'Lo, olde Grisel lyst to ryme and playe!'

Nay, Scogan, say not so, for I m'excuse —
God helpe me so! — in no rym, dowteles,
Ne thynke I never of slep to wake my muse,

22–8: drowe] *prompted*   ywroken] *avenged*   figure] *shape*   cure] *care*
29–35: wreche] *vengeance*   hoor] *grey*   rounde] *rotund*   so lykly] *so
(im)probable*   mede] *reward*   Grisel] *Greybeard*

145

That rusteth in my shethe stille in pees.
While I was yong, I put hir forth in prees;   40
But al shal passe that men prose or ryme;
Take every man hys turn, as for his tyme.

Envoy

Scogan, that knelest at the stremes hed
Of grace, of alle honour and worthynesse,
In th'ende of which strem I am dul as ded,
Forgete in solytarie wildernesse —
Yet, Scogan, thenke on Tullius kyndenesse;
Mynne thy frend, there it may fructyfye!
Far-wel, and loke thow never eft Love dyffye.

39–42: shethe] *sheath (? – odd mixed metaphor)*   in prees] *in public*
43–9: the stremes hed] *the Head of the Thames at Windsor*   th'ende] *the
mouth*   Tullius] *Roman king renowned for his charity*   Mynne] *remember*
fructyfye] *bear fruit*

The Canterbury Tales

∿

T*he Canterbury Tales* is Chaucer's greatest and most original poem, and the work with which his name was primarily associated from the first. It is his last substantial work, taking up much of his activity in the last twelve years or so of his life, and nothing in his previous output would lead us to expect it. The *General Prologue* describes how this diverse group of pilgrims from London to Canterbury came together by chance ('by aventure yfalle / In felaweshipe' (24–5)) and agreed to while away the time (something they probably should not be doing on a pilgrimage) by telling stories. Although there were earlier collections of stories, extending back to the *Arabian Nights* and similar anthologies, and some in the recent past like Boccaccio's *Decameron*, the way Chaucer links the tellers and their tales was a new and much more ambitious strategy. The ambition was beyond the capacity of any writer to complete: the plan as set out by the Host in the Tabard Inn in Southwark at the outset would require 120-odd stories, and as the narrative developed Chaucer introduced a complex and dramatic set of relationships between the pilgrims as they tell stories to 'quit' (requite) each other and argue about life and morality. The grand claims made for Chaucer – that he was 'the father of English literature', and that 'here is God's plenty' in Dryden's words – are securely founded here. The *Tales* might also be said to be 'unfinished but complete' (as was said of *The Faerie Queene*) because we have the *General Prologue* that sets the pilgrimage in motion, the grave moral conclusion of *The Parson's Tale* and the 'Retractions' that follow it, and plenty of the intervening stories and exchanges between the characters to satisfy us as we read. We begin with the opening of the *General Prologue*, one of the most celebrated openings in English literature, echoed from Chaucer's own time to *The Waste Land* and beyond.

General Prologue

Whan that Aprill with his shoures soote
The droghte of March hath perced to the roote,
And bathed every veyne in swich licour
Of which vertu engendred is the flour;
Whan Zephirus ek with his sweete breeth
Inspired hath in every holt and heeth
The tendre croppes, and the yonge sonne

1–7: shoures soote] *showers sweet*   droghte] *drought*   perced] *pierced*   veyne] *vine*   Of which vertu] *by which power*   Whan Zephirus ek] *the West Wind too*   holt and heeth] *wood and landscape*   tendre croppes] *young crops*

Hath in the Ram his halve cours yronne,
And smale foweles maken melodye,
That slepen al the nyght with open ye   10
(So priketh hem nature in hir corages);
Thanne longen folk to goon on pilgrimages,
And palmeres for to seken straunge strondes,
To ferne halwes, kowthe in sondry londes;
And specially from every shires ende
Of Engelond to Caunterbury they wende,
The hooly blisful martir for to seke,
That hem hath holpen whan that they were seeke.
Bifil that in that seson on a day,
In Southwerk at the Tabard as I lay   20
Redy to wenden on my pilgrymage
To Caunterbury with ful devout corage,
At nyght was come into that hostelrye
Wel nyne and twenty in a compaignye,
Of sondry folk, by aventure yfalle
In felaweshipe, and pilgrimes were they alle,
That toward Caunterbury wolden ryde.

8-10: his halve cours] *half of his course*   smale foweles] *little birds*   open ye]
eyes open
11-20: priketh] *urges*   corages] *libido*   strondes] *coastlines*   ferne halwes]
foreign shrines   kowthe] *known*   shires ende] *county's end*   wende] *go*
blisful] *blessed*   holpen] *helped*   seeke] *sick*   Bifil] *It so happened*   the
Tabard] *the Tabard Inn*
21-7: wenden] *go*   devout corage] *pious disposition*   Wel] *fully*   sondry]
various   aventure yfalle] *chance fallen*   In felaweshipe] *together*

149

The chambres and the stables weren wyde,
And wel we weren esed atte beste.
And shortly, whan the sonne was to reste,   30
So hadde I spoken with hem everichon
That I was of hir felaweshipe anon,
And made forward erly for to ryse,
To take oure wey ther as I yow devyse.

But nathelees, whil I have tyme and space,
Er that I ferther in this tale pace,
Me thynketh it acordaunt to resoun
To telle yow al the condicioun
Of ech of hem, so as it semed me,
And whiche they weren, and of what degree,   40
And ek in what array that they were inne;
And at a knyght than wol I first bigynne.

A Knyght ther was, and that a worthy man,
That fro the tyme that he first bigan
To riden out, he loved chivalrie,
Trouthe and honour, fredom and curteisie.

28–30: chambres] *bedrooms*   wyde] *spacious*   esed] *accommodated*   to reste]
gone down
31–4: everichon] *everyone*   of hir felaweshipe] *accepted by them*   forward]
agreement   take] *make*   devyse   *describe*
35–42: pace] *proceed*   condicioun] *circumstances*   degree] *status*   array] *dress*
43–6: fredom] *honour*

Ful worthy was he in his lordes werre,
And therto hadde he riden, no man ferre,
As wel in cristendom as in hethenesse,
And evere honoured for his worthynesse.   50
At Alisaundre he was whan it was wonne.
Ful ofte tyme he hadde the bord bigonne
Aboven alle nacions in Pruce;
In Lettow hadde he reysed and in Ruce,
No cristen man so ofte of his degree.
In Gernade at the seege ek hadde he be
Of Algezir, and riden in Belmarye.
At Lyeys was he and at Satalye,
Whan they were wonne; and in the Grete See
At many a noble armee hadde he be.   60
At mortal batailles hadde he been fiftene,
And foughten for oure feith at Tramyssene
In lystes thries, and ay slayn his foo.
This ilke worthy knyght hadde been also
Somtyme with the lord of Palatye
Agayn another hethen in Turkye.

47–50: werre] *war*   ferre] *further*   hethenesse] *pagan lands*
51–60: Alisaundre] *Alexandria*   bord bigonne] *sat at the head*   Pruce] *Prussia*
Lettow] *Lithuania*   reysed] *ridden to battle*   Ruce] *Russia*   Gernade]
Granada   Algezir] *Algeciras*   Belmarye] *Benmarin (in Morocco)*   Lyeys] *Ayash*
(in Turkey)   Satalye] *Atalia (in Turkey)*   Grete See] *Mediterranean*
61–6: Tramyssene] *Tlemcen (in Algeria)*   lystes] *knightly duels*   Palatye] *Balat*
(in Turkey)

And everemoore he hadde a sovereyn prys;
And though that he were worthy, he was wys,
And of his port as meeke as is a mayde.
He nevere yet no vileynye ne sayde   70
In al his lyf unto no maner wight.
He was a verray, parfit gentil knyght.
But, for to tellen yow of his array,
His hors were goode, but he was nat gay.
Of fustian he wered a gypon
Al bismotered with his habergeon,
For he was late ycome from his viage,
And wente for to doon his pilgrymage . . .

Ther was also a Nonne, a Prioresse,
That of hir smylyng was ful symple and coy;
Hire gretteste ooth was but by Seinte Loy;
And she was cleped madame Eglentyne.
Ful weel she soong the service dyvyne,
Entuned in hir nose ful semely;
And Frenssh she spak ful faire and fetisly,

67–70: prys] *reputation*   port] *bearing*   vileynye] *rudeness*
71–8: wight] *person*   verray] *true*   parfit gentil] *perfectly noble*   array]
dress   gay] *richly dressed*   fustian] *coarse cloth*   gypon] *tunic*   bismotered]
stained   habergeon] *coat of mail*   viage] *travels*
1–7: symple and coy] *modest and shy*   ooth] *oath*   madame Eglentyne] *Lady
Sweetbriar*   soong] *sang*   Entuned] *intoned*   fetisly] *elegantly*

After the scole of Stratford atte Bowe,
For Frenssh of Parys was to hire unknowe.
At mete wel ytaught was she with alle;   10
She leet no morsel from hir lippes falle,
Ne wette hir fyngres in hir sauce depe;
Wel koude she carie a morsel and wel kepe
That no drope ne fille upon hire brist.
In curteisie was set ful muchel hir list.
Hir over-lippe wyped she so clene
That in hir coppe ther was no ferthyng sene
Of grece, whan she dronken hadde hir draughte.
Ful semely after hir mete she raughte.
And sikerly she was of greet desport,   20
And ful plesaunt, and amyable of port,
And peyned hire to countrefete cheere
Of court, and to been estatlich of manere,
And to ben holden digne of reverence.
But for to speken of hire conscience,
She was so charitable and so pitous
She wolde wepe, if that she saugh a mous

8–10: At mete] *when eating*

11–20: kepe] *take care*   brist] *breast*   list] *inclination*   over-lippe] *top
lip*   ferthyng] *morsel*   after hir mete she raughte] *she reached out for her food*
greet desport] *dignified manner*   port] *bearing*

21–7: port] *bearing*   peyned hire] *took pains*   cheere] *manners*   digne]
worthy   conscience] *ethics*   pitous] *sympathetic*

Kaught in a trappe, if it were deed or bledde.
Of smale houndes hadde she that she fedde
With rosted flessh, or milk and wastel-breed.   30
But soore wepte she if oon of hem were deed,
Or if men smoot it with a yerde smerte;
And al was conscience and tendre herte.
Ful semyly hir wympul pynched was,
Hir nose tretys, hir eyen greye as glas,
Hir mouth ful smal, and therto softe and reed.
But sikerly she hadde a fair forheed;
It was almoost a spanne brood, I trowe;
For, hardily, she was nat undergrowe.
Ful fetys was hir cloke, as I was war.   40
Of smal coral aboute hire arm she bar
A peire of bedes, gauded al with grene,
And theron heng a brooch of gold ful sheene,
On which ther was first write a crowned A,
And after *Amor vincit omnia* . . .

28–30: wastel-breed] *fine white bread*
31–40: deed] *dead*   yerde] *whip*   smerte] *hard*   semyly] *fittingly*   pynched]
pleated   tretys] *well-shaped*   greye] *pale blue*   sikerly] *certainly*   spanne]
about eight inches   trowe] *believe*   hardily] *certainly*   fetys] *elegant*
41–5: gauded] *divided*   sheene] *sparkling*   Amor vincit omnia] *Love overcomes
everything*

A Monk ther was, a fair for the maistrie,
An outridere, that lovede venerie,
A manly man, to been an abbot able.
Ful many a deyntee hors hadde he in stable,
And whan he rood, men myghte his brydel heere
Gynglen in a whistlynge wynd als cleere
And ek as loude as dooth the chapel belle
Ther as this lord was kepere of the celle.
The reule of Seint Maure or of Seint Beneit,
By cause that it was old and somdel streit   10
This ilke monk leet olde thynges pace,
And heeld after the newe world the space.
He yaf nat of that text a pulled hen,
That seith that hunters ben nat hooly men,
Ne that a monk, whan he is recchelees,
Is likned til a fissh that is waterlees, –
This is to seyn, a monk out of his cloystre.
But thilke text heeld he nat worth an oystre;
And I seyde his opinion was good.
What sholde he studie and make hymselven wood,   20

1–10: a fair] *an exceptionally good one*   maistrie] *social dominance*   outridere]
travelling official   venerie] *hunting*   manly] *powerful*   deyntee] *fine*
Gynglen] *jingling*   Ther] *where*   celle] *lesser monastery*   Seinte Maure]
St Maurus   Seint Beneit] *St Benedict*   somdel streit] *rather strict*
11–20: ilke] *same*   leet olde thynges pace] *let old practices go*   heeld . . . the
space] *kept to the fashion*   yaf] *gave*   of] *for*   pulled] *plucked*   recchelees]
outside of the Rule   likned til a fissh that is waterlees] *like a fish out of water*
nat worth an oystre] *worthless*   What] *Why*   wood] *crazy*

Upon a book in cloystre alwey to poure,
Or swynken with his hands, and laboure,
As Austyn bit? How shal the world be served? . . .

A Clerk ther was of Oxenford also,
That unto logyk hadde longe ygo.
As leene was his hors as is a rake,
And he nas nat right fat, I undertake,
But looked holwe, and therto sobrely.
Ful thredbare was his overeste courtepy;
For he hadde geten hym yet no benefice,
Ne was so worldly for to have office.
For hym was levere have at his beddes heed
Twenty bookes, clad in blak or reed,   10
Of Aristotle and his philosophie,
Than robes riche, or fithele, or gay sautrie.
But al be that he was a philosophre,
Yet hadde he but litel gold in cofre;
But al that he myghte of his freendes hente,
On bookes and on lernynge he it spente,
And bisily gan for the soules preye

21–3: swynken] *work*   Austyn] *St Augustine*
1–10: Clerk] *scholar*   Oxenford] *Oxford*   ygo] *devoted himself*   leene] *thin*
right] *very*   undertake] *declare*   holwe] *thin*   sobrely] *serious*   overeste
courtepy]*overcoat*   benefice] *clerical living*   office] *a job*   hym was levere]
he'd prefer   clad] *bound*
11–17: fithele] *a fiddle*   gay sautrie] *elegant psalter*   al be] *even though*
philosophre] *thinker*   cofre] *chest*   hente] *get*

156

Of hem that yaf hym wherwith to scoleye.
Of studie took he moost cure and moost heede,
Noght o word spak he moore than was neede,   20
And that was seyd in forme and reverence,
And short and quyk and ful of hy sentence;
Sownynge in moral vertu was his speche,
And gladly wolde he lerne and gladly teche . . .

A Frankeleyn was in his compaignye.
Whit was his berd as is the dayesye;
Of his complexioun he was sangwyn.
Wel loved he by the morwe a sop in wyn;
To lyven in delit was evere his wone,
For he was Epicurus owene sone,
That heeld opinioun that pleyn delit
Was verray felicitee parfit.
An housholdere, and that a greet, was he;
Seint Julian he was in his contree.   10
His breed, his ale, was alweys after oon;

18–20: yaf hym wherwyth to scoleye] *paid for his studies*   cure] *care*
neede] *necessary*
21–4: in forme and reverence] *formally and respectfully*   short] *brief*   hy
sentence] *exalted moral content*   Sownynge in] *consistent with*
1–10: dayesye] *daisy*   complexioun] *temperament*   sangwyn] *cheerful*   by the
morwe] *in the morning*   sop] *bit of bread*   wone] *habit*   Epicurus owene
sone] *an Epicurean*   pleyn delit] *pure pleasure*   verray] *true*   felicitee parfit]
perfect happiness   housholdere] *owner of a big house*   Seint Julian] *the host*
contree] *part of the country*]
11: always after oon] *unvaryingly good*

A better envyned man was nowher noon.

Withoute bake mete was nevere his hous

Of fissh and flessh, and that so plentevous,

It snewed in his hous of mete and drynke,

Of alle deyntees that men koude thynke.

After the sondry sesons of the yeer,

So chaunged he his mete and his soper.

Ful many a fat partrich hadde he in muwe,

And many a breem and many a luce in stuwe . . .   20

A good Wif was ther of biside Bathe,

But she was somdel deef, and that was scathe.

Of clooth-makyng she hadde swich an haunt,

She passed hem of Ypres and of Gaunt.

In al the parisshe wif ne was ther noon

That to the offrynge bifore hire sholde goon;

And if ther dide, certeyn so wrooth was she,

That she was out of alle charitee.

Hir coverchiefs ful fyne weren of ground;

I dorste swere they weyeden ten pound   10

That on a Sonday weren upon hir heed.

12–20: envyned] *cellared*   mete] *pie*   flessh] *meat*   plentevous] *plenti-*
ful   snewed] *snowed*   deyntees] *delicacies*   After] *according to*   sondry]
various   muwe] *pen*   breem] *bream*   luce *pike*   stuwe] *fish-pond*
1–11: somdel] *slightly*   deef] *deaf*   scathe] *a pity*   haunt] *skill*   Gaunt]
Ghent   offrynge] *gift-offering at Mass*   wrooth] *angry*   out of alle charitee]
very put out   coverchiefs] *scarves*   fyne . . . of ground] *fine in texture*   dorste
swere] *dare swear*   weyeden] *weighed*

Hir hosen weren of fyn scarlet reed,
Ful streite yteyd, and shoes ful moyste and newe.
Boold was hir face, and fair, and reed of hewe.
She was a worthy womman al hir lyve:
Housbondes at chirche dore she hadde fyve,
Withouten oother compaignye in youthe, –
But therof nedeth nat to speke as nowthe.
And thries hadde she been at Jerusalem;
She hadde passed many a straunge strem . . .   20

The Reve was a sclendre colerik man.
His berd was shave as ny as ever he kan;
His heer was by his erys ful round yshorn;
His top was dokked lyk a preest biforn.
Ful longe were his legges and ful lene,
Ylyk a staf, ther was no calf ysene.
Wel koude he kepe a gerner and a bynne;
Ther was noon auditour koude on him wynne.
Wel wiste he by the droghte and by the reyn
The yeldynge of his seed and of his greyn.   10

12–20: hosen] *stockings*   streite yteyd] *laced tightly*   moyste] *soft-leathered*
Boold] *healthy*   a worthy womman] *a woman of substance*   at chirche dore] *at
the church door*   Withouten] *not to mention*   as nowthe] *for now*
thries] *three times*   straunge strem] *foreign sea*
1–10: sclendre] *thin*   colerik] *bad-tempered*   shave] *shaved*   ny] *close*
yshorn] *close-cropped*   top] *head*   biforn] *at the front*   lene] *thin*   staf] *stick*
garner] *granary*   bynne] *corn-bin*   auditour] *surveyor*   droghte] *dryness*
yeldynge] *yield*

His lordes sheep, his neet, his dayerye,
His swyn, his hors, his stoor, and his pultrye
Was hoolly in this reves governynge,
And by his covenant yaf the rekenynge,
Syn that his lord was twenty yeer of age.
Ther koude no man brynge hym in arrerage.
Ther nas baillif, ne hierde, nor oother hyne,
That he ne knew his sleighte and his covyne;
They were adrad of hym as of the deeth.
His wonyng was ful faire upon an heeth . . .   20

A Somonour was ther with us in that place,
That hadde a fyr-reed cherubynnes face,
For saucefleem he was, with eyen narwe.
As hoot he was and lecherous as a sparwe,
With scalled browes blake and piled berd.
Of his visage children were aferd.
Ther nas quyk-silver, lytarge, ne brymstoon,
Boras, ceruce, ne oille of tartre noon,
Ne oynement that wolde clense and byte,

11–20: neet] *cattle*   dayerye] *dairy*   stoor] *stock*   covenant] *contract*
rekenynge] *audit*   arrerage] *arrears*   hierde] *herdsman*   hyne] *servant*
sleighte] *trickery*   covyne] *treachery*
1–9: Somonour] *bailiff of a Church court*   fyr-reed] *fire-red*   cherubynnes]
cherub's   saucefleem] *pimpled*   eyen narwe] *little eyes*   scalled] *scorbutic*
piled] *thin*   quyk-silver] *mercury*   lytarge] *lead monoxide*   Boras] *borax*
ceruce] *white lead*   oille of tarter] *cream of tartar*   byte] *burn off*

That hym myghte helpen of his whelkes white,   10
Nor of the knobbes sittynge on his chekes.
Wel loved he garleek, oynons, and ek lekes,
And for to drynken strong wyn, reed as blood;
Thanne wolde he speke and crie as he were wood.
And whan that he wel dronken hadde the wyn,
Thanne wolde he speke no word but latyn.
A fewe termes hadde he, two or thre,
That he had lerned out of som decree –
No wonder is, he herde it al the day;
And ek ye knowen wel how that a jay   20
Kan clepen 'Watte!' as wel as kan the pope.
But whoso koude in oother thyng hym grope,
Thanne had he spent al his philosophie . . .

With hym ther rood a gentil Pardoner
Of Rouncivale, his freend and his compeer,
That streight was comen fro the court of Rome.
Ful loude he soong 'Com hider, love, to me!'
This somonour bar to hym a stif burdoun;
Was nevere trompe of half so greet a soun.

10–20: whelkes] *pustules*   knobbes] *boils*   crie] *shout*   wood] *mad*   latyn]
Latin   termes] *technical terms*   decree] *Church decretal*
21–3: Watte] *Walt(er)*   oother] *further*   grope] *examine*
1–6: Pardoner] *licensed seller of Indulgences*   Rouncivale] *Hospital at Charing
Cross*   compeer] *friend*   the court of Rome] *the Papal court*   'Com hider,
love, to me'] *(a popular love-song)*   stif burdoun] *loud bass*   trompe] *trumpet*
soun] *sound*

This pardoner hadde heer as yelow as wex,
But smothe it heeng as dooth a strike of flex;
By ounces henge his lokkes that he hadde,
And therwith he his shuldres overspradde;   10
But thynne it lay, by colpons oon and oon.
But hood, for jolitee, wered he noon,
For it was trussed up in his walet.
Hym thoughte he rood al of the newe jet;
Dischevelee, save his cappe, he rood al bare.
Swiche glarynge eyen hadde he as an hare.
A vernycle hadde he sowed upon his cappe.
His walet lay biforn hym in his lappe,
Bretful of pardoun, comen from Rome al hoot.
A voys he hadde as smal as hath a goot . . .   20

The Author makes his excuses:

But first I pray yow, of youre curteisye,
That ye n' arette it nat my vileynye,
Thogh that I pleynly speke in this mateere,

7–10: heer] *hair*   wex] *wax*   heeng] *hung*   strike of flex] *hank of flax*
ounces] *thin strands*
11–20: colpons] *wisps*   oon and oon] *one by one*   jolitee] *attractiveness*
trussed] *wrapped*   walet] *bag*   of the newe jet] *in the latest fashion*
Dischevelee] *with hair loose*   glarynge eyen] *staring eyes*   vernycle] *badge of*
St Veronica's cloth   lappe] *pocket*   Bretful] *full to the brim*   smal] *high-pitched*
goot] *goat*
1–3: of youre curteisye] *by your good will*   n'arette it nat my vileynye] *don't see it*
as my ignorance   pleynly] *explicitly*

162

To telle yow hir wordes and hir cheere,
Ne thogh I speke hir wordes proprely.
For this ye knowen al so wel as I,
Whoso shal telle a tale after a man,
He moot reherce as ny as evere he kan
Everich a word, if it be in his charge,
Al speke he never so rudeliche and large,   10
Or ellis he moot telle his tale untrewe,
Or feyne thyng, or fynde wordes newe.
He may nat spare, althogh he were his brother;
He moot as wel seye o word as another.
Crist spak hymself ful brode in hooly writ,
And wel ye woot no vileynye is it.
Ek Plato seith, whoso that kan hym rede,
The wordes moote be cosyn to the dede.
Also I prey yow to foryeve it me,
Al have I nat set folk in hir degree   20
Heere in this tale, as that they sholde stonde.
My wit is short, ye may wel understonde.

4–10: hir cheere] *their behaviour* proprely] *accurately* Whoso shal] *whoever
has to* reherce as ny] *repeat as closely* 9–10: Everich] *every* charge] *duty*
Al] *even if* rudeliche] *crudely*
11–20: moot] *must* untrewe] *inaccurately* feyne thyng] *make something up*
spare] *forbear* o] *one* brode] *plainly* ye woot] *you know* kan hym rede]
can interpret him cosyn] *related* Al] *if* degree] *social rank*
21–2: ye may wel understonde] *as you can imagine*

The 'true, perfectly courteous knight' tells a version of Boccac-
cio's *Teseida*, the epic of Theseus. It tells how Theseus has to
resolve a dispute between 'two noble kinsmen' (as in Shakespeare's
version), Palamon and Arcite, who are both in love with the same
lady, Emelye. Palamon is a votive of 'Diane the chaste', goddess of
chastity, and prays in a temple dedicated to her; Arcite is a follower
of Mars, the violent god of war, and prays in his temple, the wall-
depictions of which are described in this ferocious passage (1967ff).

Why sholde I noght as wel ek telle yow al
The portreiture that was upon the wal
Withinne the temple of myghty Mars the rede?
Al peynted was the wal, in lengthe and brede,
Lyk to the estres of the grisly place
That highte the grete temple of Mars in Trace,
In thilke colde, frosty regioun
Ther as Mars hath his sovereyn mansioun.
First on the wal was peynted a forest,
In which ther dwelleth neither man ne best,   10
With knotty, knarry, bareyne trees olde,
Of stubbes sharpe and hidouse to biholde,

1–10: as wel] *also* rede] *red* brede] *breadth* estres] *apartments* grisly] *hideous* highte] *was called* Trace] *Thrace* thilke] *that same* sovereyn mansioun] *principal habitation*
11–12: knarry] *gnarled* bareyne] *dead* stubbes] *stumps*

In which ther ran a rumbel in a swough,
As though a storm sholde bresten every bough.
And dounward from an hille, under a bente,
Ther stood the temple of Mars armypotente,
Wroght al of burned steel, of which the entree
Was long and streit, and gastly for to see.
And therout came a rage and swich a veze
That it made al the gate for to rese.   20
The northren lyght in at the dores shoon,
For wyndowe on the wal ne was ther noon,
Thurgh which men myghten any light discerne.
The dore was al of adamant eterne,
Yclenched overthwart and endelong
With iren tough; and for to make it strong,
Every pyler, the temple to sustene,
Was tonne-greet, of iren bright and shene.
Ther saugh I first the derke ymaginyng
Of Felonye, and al the compassyng;   30
The crueel Ire, reed as any gleede;
The pykepurs, and ek the pale Drede;

13–20: rumbel] *rumble*   swough] *wind*   bresten] *break*   bente] *grassy slope*
burned] *burnished*   streit] *narrow*   gastly] *hideous*   rage] *rush*
veze] *blast of wind*   rese] *shake*
21–30: northren lyght] *light from the north*   eterne] *everlasting*   Yclenched
over thwart and endelong] *fastened in breadth and length*   tough] *hard*   pyler]
pillar   sustene] *support*   tonne-greet] *wide as a barrel*   shene] *shining*
derke ymaginyng] *hidden scheming*   Felonye] *Evil*   compassyng] *plotting*
31–2: Ire] *Anger*   gleede] *coal*   pykepurs] *pickpocket*   Drede] *Fear*

The smylere with the knyf under the cloke;
The shepne brennynge with the blake smoke;
The tresoun of the mordrynge in the bedde;
The open werre, with woundes al bibledde;
Contek, with blody knyf and sharp manace.
Al ful of chirkyng was that sory place.
The sleere of hymself yet saugh I ther, –
His herte-blood hath bathed al his heer;   40
The nayl ydryven in the shode a-nyght;
The colde deeth, with mouth gapyng upright.
Amyddes of the temple sat Meschaunce,
With disconfort and sory contenaunce.
Yet saugh I Woodnesse, laughynge in his rage,
Armed Compleint, Outhees, and fiers Outrage;
The careyne in the busk, with throte ycorve;
A thousand slayn, and nat of qualm ystorve;
The tiraunt, with the pray by force yraft;
The toun destroyed, ther was no thyng laft.   50

33–40: shepne] *stable*   tresoun] *treachery*   mordrynge] *murder*   with woundes
al bibledde] *blood-covered from wounds*   Contek] *Strife*   manace *threat*
chirkyng] *groaning*   sory] *sorrowful*   sleere of hymself] *suicide*
bathed] *soaked*
41–50: shode] *head-crown*   upright] *upwards*   Amyddes] *In the middle*
Meschaunce] *Misfortune*   disconfort] *distress*   sory] *sorrowful*   Woodnesse]
Madness   rage] *raving*   Compleint] *Grievance*   Outhees] *Outcry*   Outrage]
Savagery   careyne] *corpse*   busk] *bush*   ycorve] *cut*   of qualm ystorve] *killed
by plague*   pray] *prey*   yraft] *taken off*

Yet saugh I brent the shippes hoppesteres;
The hunte strangled with the wilde beres;
The sowe freten the child right in the cradel;
The cook yscalded, for al his longe ladel.
Noght was foryeten by the infortune of Marte
The cartere overryden with his carte:
Under the wheel ful lowe he lay adoun.
Ther were also, of Martes divisioun,
The barbour, and the bocher, and the smyth,
That forgeth sharpe swerdes on his styth.   60
And al above, depeynted in a tour,
Saugh I Conquest, sittynge in greet honour,
With the sharpe swerd over his heed
Hangynge by a soutil twynes threed.
Depeynted was the slaughtre of Julius,
Of grete Nero, and of Antonius;
Al be that thilke tyme they were unborn,
Yet was hir deth depeynted ther-biforn
By manasynge of Mars, right by figure.
So was it shewed in that portreiture,   70

51-60: brent] *burnt*   hoppesteres] *dancers (?)*   hunte] *hunter*   strangled]
crushed   beres] *bears*   sowe freten] *sow devouring*   for al] *in spite of*
infortune of Marte] *ill-influence of Mars*   overryden] *run over*
Martes divisioun] *Mars' party*   bocher] *butcher*   styth] *anvil*
61-70: depeynted] *painted*   soutil twynes threed] *slender thread of twine*
Julius] *Julius Caesar*   Antonius] *Mark Antony*   manasynge] *threatening*   by
figure] *through representation*

As is depeynted in the sterres above
Who shal be slayn or elles deed for love.
Suffiseth oon ensample in stories olde;
I may nat rekene hem alle though I wolde.
The statue of Mars upon a carte stood
Armed, and looked grym as he were wood;
And over his heed ther shynen two figures
Of sterres, that been cleped in scriptures,
That oon Puella, that oother Rubeus –
This god of armes was arrayed thus.   80
A wolf ther stood biforn hym at his feet
With eyen rede, and of a man he eet;
With soutil pencel depeynted was this storie
In redoutynge of Mars and of his glorie.

The gods argue out the relative rights of Mars and Venus; but
Venus' father Saturn declares that he has the real power (2453ff).

'My deere doghter Venus', quod Saturne,
'My cours, that hath so wyde for to turne,
Hath moore power than woot any man.
Myn is the drenchyng in the see so wan;

71–80: ensample] *exemplary case*   stories] *histories*   carte] *chariot*   wood] *mad*
sterres] *stars*   Puella . . . Rubeus] *(figures in Astrology)*
81–8: eet] *ate*   soutil pencel] *fine pen*   redoutynge] *reverence*   quod] *said*
cours] *sphere of influence*   woot] *knows*   Myn] *my responsibility*
drenchyng] *drowning*   wan] *pale*

Myn is the prison in the derke cote;

Myn is the stranglyng and hangyng by the throte,   90

The murmure and the cherles rebellyng,

The groynynge, and the pryvee empoysonyng;

I do vengeance and pleyn correccioun,

Whil I dwelle in the signe of the Leoun.

Myn is the ruyne of the hye halles,

The fallynge of the toures and of the walles

Upon the mynour or the carpenter.

I slow Sampsoun, shakynge the piler;

And myne be the maladyes colde,

The derke tresons, and the castes olde;   100

My lookyng is the fader of pestilence.

The gods come to a resolution, more satisfactory for them than for the hapless humans they represent. Arcite, who prayed to Mars, wins the battle which entitles him to Emelye; but his horse rears when it is frightened by an 'infernal fury' sent by Pluto, and Arcite falls to his death. The coast is now clear for Palamon, who prayed to the goddess of love, to marry Emelye and live happily ever after. With his dying words, Arcite commits her to Palamon, reflecting famously on the transience of things:

89–90: cote] *cell*

91–100: murmure] *complaining*   cherles] *peasants'*   groynynge] *grumbling*
pryvee] *secret*   correccioun] *punishment*   the signe of the Leoun] *the
constellation Leo*   mynour] *miner*   tresons] *plots*
101: lookyng] *astronomical aspect*

'What is this world? What asketh men to have?
Now with his love, now in his colde grave
Allone withouten any compaignye!' (2777–9)

The non-description of his funeral is given forty-three lines of
recusatio or *occupatio*, the rhetorical figure by which a substantial
description is given of what will not be mentioned (2919ff).

But how the fyr was maked upon highte,
Ne ek the names that the trees highte,
As ook, firre, birch, aspe, alder, holm, popler,
Wylugh, elm, plane, assh, box, chasteyn, lynde, laurer,
Mapul, thorn, bech, hasel, ew, whippeltree,
How they weren feld, shal nat be toold for me;
Ne hou the goddes ronnen up and doun,
Disherited of hire habitacioun,
In which they woneden in reste and pees,   110
Nymphes, fawnes and amadrides;
Ne hou the beestes and the briddes alle
Fledden for fere, whan the wode was falle;
Ne how the ground agast was of the light,
That was nat wont to seen the sonne bright;
Ne how the fyr was couched first with stree,
And thanne with drye stikkes cloven a thre,

102–10: highte] *were called*   aspe] *aspen*   holm] *holm-oak*   Wylugh] *willow*
chasteyn] *chestnut*   lynde] *lime*   laurer] *laurel*   bech] *beech*   whippeltree]
dogwood   feld] *felled*   Disherited] *disinherited*   woneden] *had lived*
111–7: Nymphes] *wood-nymphs*   agast . . . of] *frightened by*   couched] *laid*
stree] *straw*   cloven a thre] *cut in three*

And thanne with grene wode and spicerye,
And thanne with clooth of gold and with perrye,
And gerlandes, hangynge with ful many a flour;   120
The mirre, th' encens, with al so greet odour;
Ne how Arcite lay among al this,
Ne what richesse aboute his body is;
Ne how that Emelye, as was the gyse,
Putte in the fyr of funeral servyse;
Ne how she swowned whan men made the fyr,
Ne what she spak, ne what was hir desir;
Ne what jeweles men in the fyre caste,
Whan that the fyr was greet and brente faste;
Ne how somme caste hir sheeldd, and somme hir spere,   130
And of hire vestimentz, whiche that they were,
And coppes fulle of wyn, and milk, and blood,
Into the fyr, that brente as it were wood;
Ne how the Grekes, with an huge route,
Thries riden al the fyr aboute
Upon the left hand, with a loud shoutynge,
And thries with hir speres claterynge;
And thries how the ladyes gonne crye;
Ne how that lad was homward Emelye;
Ne how Arcite is brent to asshen colde;   140

118–20: spicerye] *mixed spices*   perrye] *precious stones*
121–30: mirre] *myrr*   gyse] *practice*   Putte in] *entrusted to*   swowned] *fainted*
brente faste] *burned fiercely*
131–40: vestimentz] *clothes*   route] *throng*   Thries] *three times*   lad] *led*

Ne how that lyche-wake was yholde
Al thilke nyght; ne how the Grekes pleye
The wake-pleyes, ne kepe I nat to seye;
Who wrastleth best naked with oille enoynt,
Ne who that baar hym best, in no disjoynt.
I wol nat tellen ek how that they goon
Hoom til Atthenes, whan the pley is doon;
But shortly to the point thanne wol I wende,
And maken of my longe tale an ende.

The Miller's Tale

The Miller – a man who, we know from the *General Prologue*, could break any door by running at it with his head – tells a tale of seduction and scurrility. Here the aged carpenter John is concerned for his student-lodger Nicholas, afraid that too much studying has damaged his mind. In fact Nicholas is constructing an extremely complicated, Heath Robinson plan to have sex with the carpenter's nubile young wife, Alison. John and his muscular servant break into Nicholas's room and find him transfixed (3448ff).

This carpenter to blessen hym bigan,
And seyde 'Help us, Seinte Frydeswyde!
A man woot litel what hym shal bityde.

141–9: lyche-wake] *body-wake*   wake-pleyes] *funeral games*   disjoynt] *difficulty*
1–3: Seinte Frydeswyde] *St Frideswide (an Oxford healer)*   woot litel] *little knows*
bityde] *befall*

This man is falle, with his astromye,
In some woodnesse or in som agonye.
I thoghte ay wel how that it sholde be!
Men sholde nat knowe of Goddes pryvetee.
Ye, blessed be alwey a lewed man
That noght but oonly his bileve kan!
So ferde another clerk with astromye;   10
He walked in the feeldes, for to prye
Upon the sterres, what ther sholde bifalle,
Til he was in a marle-pit yfalle;
He saugh nat that. But yet, by Seint Thomas,
Me reweth soore of hende Nicholas.
He shal be rated of his studiyng,
If that I may, by Jhesus, hevene kyng!
Get me a staf, that I may underspore,
Whil that thou, Robyn, hevest up the dore.
He shal out of his studiyng, as I gesse –'   20
And to the chambre dore he gan hym dresse.
His knave was a strong carl for the nones,

4-10: falle] *fallen*   astromye] *astronomy*   woodnesse] *madness*   thoghte ay
wel] *always knew well*
Goddes pryvetee] *God's secrets*   lewed] *ignorant*   oonly his bileve kan]
knows nothing but his creed   ferde] *fared*   clerk] *scholar*
11-20: prye] *gaze*   what ther sholde bifalle] *to predict what would happen*   Me
reweth soore of] *I'm very sorry for*   hende] *noble*   rated] *scolded*   If that I
may] *if I can*   underspore] *prop up*   hevest] *lift*   shal out] *will (get) out*
21-2: dresse] *approach*   for the nones] *indeed*

And by the haspe he haaf it of atones;
Into the floor the dore fil anon.
This Nicholas sat ay as stille as stoon,
And evere caped upward into the eir.
This carpenter wende he were in despeir,
And hente hym by the sholdres myghtily,
And shook hym harde, and cride spitously
'What! Nicholay! what, how! what, looke adoun!   30
Awak, and thenk on Cristes passioun!
I crouche thee from elves and fro wightes.'
Therwith the nyght-spel seyde he anon-rightes
On foure halves of the hous aboute,
And on the thresshfold of the dore withoute:
'Jhesu Crist and Seinte Benedight,
Blesse this hous from every wikked wight,
For nyghtes verye, the white *pater-noster*!
Where wentestow, Seinte Petres soster?'
And atte laste this hende Nicholas   40
Gan for to sik soore, and seyde 'Allas!
Shal al the world be lost aftsoones now?'

23–30: haaf] *heaved*   atones] *at once*   ay] *the whole time*   caped] *gaped*
wende] *thought*   hente] *seized*   spitously] *desperately*   What!] *Hey!*
looke adoun] *look down*
31–40: thenk] *meditate*   crouche] *bless (with the cross)*   elves] *evil spirits*
nyght-spel] *night-charm*   halves] *sides*   wight] *creature*   white *pater-noster*]
ill-spirit   wentestow] *did you go*   soster] *sister*   hende] *noble*
41–2: sik] *sigh*   soore] *sorely*   aftsoones now] *right now*

Nicholas's dastardly plan works, and he is lying in the carpenter's bed with Alison. She has another aspiring lover, the parish clerk Absolon who 'is always for love so woe-begone'. He guesses that the carpenter is out of the way and starts to call from outside the bedroom window (3671ff).

This Absolon ful joly was and light,
And thoghte 'Now is tyme to wake al nyght;
For sikirly I saugh hym nat stirynge
Aboute his dore, syn day bigan to sprynge.
So moot I thryve, I shal, at cokkes crowe,
Ful pryvely knokken at his wyndowe
That stant ful lowe upon his boures wal.
To Alison now wol I tellen al   50
My love-longynge, for yet I shal nat mysse
That at the leeste wey I shal hire kisse.
Som maner confort shal I have, parfay.
My mouth hath icched al this longe day;
That is a signe of kissyng atte leeste.
Al nyght me mette ek I was at a feeste.
Therfore I wol go slepe an houre or tweye,

43–50: light] *happy*   wake] *stay awake*   sikirly] *certainly*   moot] *may*   cokkes crow] *cock-crow*   pryvely] *secretly*   stant] *is*   boures] *bedroom's*
51–7: mysse] *fail*   maner] *kind of*   parfay] *indeed*   icched] *itched*   me mette ek] *I dreamed also*

And al the nyght thanne wol I wake and pleye.'
Whan that the firste cok hath crowe, anon
Up rist this joly lovere Absolon   60
And hym arraieth gay, at poynt-devys.
But first he cheweth Greyn and lycorys,
To smellen sweete, er he hadde kembd his heer.
Under his tonge a trewe-love he beer,
For therby wende he to ben gracious.
He rometh to the carpenteres hous,
And stille he stant under the shot-wyndowe –
Unto his brest it raughte, it was so lowe –
And softe he cougheth with a semy soun –
'What do ye, hony-comb, sweete Alisoun,   70
My faire bryd, my sweete cynamome?
Awaketh, lemman myn, and speketh to me!
Wel litel thynken ye upon my wo,
That for youre love I swete ther I go.
No wonder is thogh that I swelte and swete;
I moorne as dooth a lamb after the tete.
Ywis, lemman, I have swich love-longynge,

58-60: pleye] *be active*   anon] *soon*   rist] *rises*   joly] *spirited*
61-70: hym arraieth gay] *he dresses finely*   at poynt-devys] *in every detail*
Greyn] *cardamom*   kembd] *combed*   trewe-love] *true-love knot*   wende]
thought   gracious] *attractive*   rometh] *goes along*   shot-wyndowe] *hinged
window*   raughte] *reached*   cougheth] *coughs*   semy] *little*
71-7: bryd] *bird*   lemman] *sweetheart*   swete] *sweat*   swelte] *grow faint*
tete] *teat*

That lik a turtel trewe is my moornynge.
I may nat ete na moore than a mayde.'
'Go fro the wyndow, Jakke fool', she sayde;   80
'As help me god, it wol nat be "com pa me."
I love another – and elles I were to blame –
Wel bet than thee, by Jhesu, Absolon.
Go forth thy wey, or I wol caste a ston,
And lat me slepe, a twenty devel wey!'
'Allas', quod Absolon, 'and weylawey,
That trewe love was evere so yvel biset!
Thanne kysse me, syn it may be no bet,
For Jhesus love, and for the love of me.'
'Wiltow thanne go thy wey therwith?' quod she.   90
'Ye, certes, lemman', quod this Absolon.
'Thanne make thee redy', quod she, 'I come anon.'
And unto Nicholas she seyde stille,
'Now hust, and thou shalt laughen al thy fille.'
This Absolon doun sette hym on his knees
And seyde 'I am a lord at alle degrees;
For after this I hope ther cometh moore.

78–80: turtel] *turtle-dove*   Jakke fool] *jackass*
81–90: "com pa me"] *'come and kiss me'*   Go forth thy wey] *clear off*   caste]
throw   a twenty devel wey!] *for twenty devils' sake!*   yvel biset] *ill-placed*   bet]
better   therwith] *with that*
91–7: I come anon] *I'm just coming*   stille] *quietly*   hust] *hush!*   at alle
degrees] *in every way*   hope] *think*

Lemman, thy grace, and sweete bryd, thyn oore!'
The wyndow she undoth, and that in haste.
'Have do', quod she, 'com of, and speed the faste,   100
Lest that oure neighebores thee espie.'
This Absolon gan wype his mouth ful drie.
Derk was the nyght as pich, or as the cole,
And at the wyndow out she putte hir hole,
And Absolon, hym fil no bet ne wers,
But with his mouth he kiste hir naked ers
Ful savourly, er he were war of this.
Abak he stirte, and thoughte it was amys,
For wel he wiste a womman hath no berd.
He felte a thyng al rough and long yherd,   110
And seyde, 'Fy! allas! what have I do?'
'Tehee!' quod she, and clapte the wyndow to.

The Wife of Bath's Prologue

There has been much critical debate about the relative importance
of 'tellers and tales' in *The Canterbury Tales*: whether the vivid
character sketches in the *General Prologue* or the tales that they tell

---

98–100: oore] *favour*   speed the faste] *hurry up*
101–10: pich] *pitch*   hole] *backside*   ers] *arse*   savourly] *with relish*   stirte]
jumped   amys] *wrong*   wiste] *knew*   long yherd] *long-haired*
111–12: clapte] *banged*

have literary priority. But there is a third kind of narrative that comes between these two – the long 'Prologues' to their Tales told by a few of the characters, most notably the Wife of Bath whose ostensibly autobiographical Prologue outweighs her Tale, the Canon's Yeoman whose Prologue melts imperceptibly into his Tale, and the Pardoner whose Prologue and Tale are both masterpieces. Although the Wife of Bath's Prologue and Tale don't occur in the same manuscript group as the Pardoner's, the interruption of the Wife's Prologue by the Pardoner is one of the most vivid exchanges between characters on the pilgrimage. Her Prologue has a further general significance within the whole structure: the Prologue's long account of the pros and cons of marriage led at the start of the twentieth century to the suggestion that there is a sustained discussion of marriage – 'The Marriage Group' – started by the Wife of Bath, continuing (with interruptions) through the Tales of the Clerk and the Merchant, and resolved in the conciliatory Franklin's Tale with a courtly husband who is 'servant in love, and lord in mariage'.

It is not finally possible to establish a sequential narrative for the Tales as a whole because the many manuscripts don't produce a definite order. But a dramatic moment which makes a virtue of this uncertainty is the outburst from the Wife of Bath about the woe that is in marriage – an outburst that begins a new section with no textual prompting:

'Experience, though noon auctoritee
Were in this world, is right ynogh for me
To speke of wo that is in mariage;
For, lordynges, sith I twelve yeer was of age,
Thonked be God that is eterne on lyve,
Housbondes at chirche dore I have had fyve –
If I so ofte myghte have ywedded bee –
And alle were worthy men in hir degree.
But me was toold, certeyn, nat longe agoon is,
That sith that Crist ne wente nevere but onis   10
To weddyng, in the Cane of Galilee,
That by the same ensample taughte he me
That I ne sholde wedded be but ones.
Herkne ek, lo, which a sharp word for the nones,
Biside a welle, Jhesus, God and man,
Spak in repreeve of the Samaritan:
"Thou hast yhad fyve housbondes," quod he,
"And that ilke man that now hath thee
Is noght thyn housbonde," thus seyde he certeyn.
What that he mente therby, I kan nat seyn;   20

1–10: auctoritee] *written authority*   degree] *social status*   onis] *once*
11–20: Cane] *Cana*   Herkne] *listen*   for the nones] *on the occasion*   repreeve]
reproval

180

But that I axe, why that the fifthe man
Was noon housbonde to the Samaritan?
How manye myghte she have in mariage?
Yet herde I nevere tellen in myn age
Upon this nombre diffinicioun.
Men may devyne and glosen, up and doun,
But wel I woot, expres, withoute lye,
God bad us for to wexe and multiplye;
That gentil text kan I wel understonde.
Ek wel I woot, he seyde myn housbonde   30
Sholde lete fader and mooder and take to me.
But of no nombre mencion made he,
Of bigamye, or of octogamye;
Why sholde men thanne speke of it vileynye?
Lo, heere the wise kyng, daun Salomon;
I trowe he hadde wyves mo than oon.
As wolde God it leveful were unto me
To be refresshed half so ofte as he! . . .

21–30: axe] *ask*   diffinicioun] *conclusive judgement*   devyne] *speculate*
glosen] *interpret*   expres] *clearly*
31–8: lete] *leave*   octogamye] *marriage eight times*   daun] *Lord*   leveful]
lawful   refresshed] *satisfied sexually*

Virginitee is greet perfeccion,
And continence ek with devocion,
But Crist, that of perfeccion is welle,
Bad nat every wight he sholde go selle
Al that he hadde, and gyve it to the poore,
And in swich wise folwe hym and his foore.   110
He spak to hem that wolde lyve parfitly;
And lordynges, by youre leve, that am nat I.
I wol bistowe the flour of al myn age
In the actes and in fruyt of mariage.
Telle me also, to what conclusion
Were membres maad of generacion,
And of so parfit wys a wright ywroght?
Trusteth right wel, they were nat maad for noght.
Glose whoso wole, and seye bothe up and doun
That they were maked for purgacioun   120
Of uryne, and oure bothe thynges smale
Were ek to knowe a femele from a male,
And for noon oother cause – say ye no?
The experience woot wel it is noght so.

105–10: devocion] *piety*   foore] *footsteps*
111–20: parfitly] *perfectly*   conclusion] *purpose*   membres] *organs*
generacion] *procreation*   wright] *artist*   Glose] *interpret*
121–4: thynges] *organs*   experience] *practice*

So that the clerkes be nat with me wrothe,
I sey this: that they maked ben for bothe;
That is to seye, for office and for ese
Of engendrure, ther we nat God displese.
Why sholde men elles in hir bookes sette
That man shal yelde to his wyf hire dette? 130
Now wherwith sholde he make his paiement,
If he ne used his sely instrument?
Thanne were they maad upon a creature
To purge uryne, and ek for engendrure.
But I seye noght that every wight is holde,
That hath swich harneys as I to yow tolde,
To goon and usen hem in engendrure.
Thanne sholde men take of chastitee no cure.
Crist was a mayde and shapen as a man,
And many a seint, sith that the world bigan; 140
Yet lyved they evere in parfit chastitee.
I nyl envye no virginitee.
Lat hem be breed of pured whete-seed,
And lat us wyves hoten barly-breed;

125–30: engendrure] *propagation*   sette] *write*   dette] *due*
131–40: sely] *innocent*   Thanne] *thus*   holde] *obliged*   harneys] *tackle*   cure]
care   sith that] *since*
141–4: breed] *bread*   hoten] *called*   barly-breed] *coarse bread*

183

And yet with barly-breed, Mark telle kan,
Oure Lord Jhesu refresshed many a man.
In swich estaat as God hath cleped us
I wol persevere; I nam nat precius.
In wyfhod I wol use myn instrument
As frely as my Makere hath it sent.   150
If I be daungerous, God yeve me sorwe!
Myn housbonde shal it have bothe eve and morwe,
Whan that hym list come forth and paye his dette.
An housbonde I wol have – I wol nat lette –
Which shal be bothe my dettour and my thral,
And have his tribulacion withal
Upon his flessh, whil that I am his wyf.
I have the power durynge al my lyf
Upon his propre body, and noght he.
Right thus the Apostel tolde it unto me,   160
And bad oure housbondes for to love us weel.
Al this sentence me liketh every deel' –
Up stirte the Pardoner, and that anon;
'Now, dame,' quod he, 'by God and by Seint John!

145–50: cleped us] *called us to*   precius] *fastidious*   frely] *generously*
151–60: daungerous] *prohibitive*   lette] *hold back*   tribulacion] *suffering*
withal] *also*   power] *control*   propre] *own*
161–4: deel] *bit*   stirte] *started*   anon] *straightaway*

Ye been a noble prechour in this cas.

I was aboute to wedde a wyf; allas!

What sholde I bye it on my flessh so deere?

Yet hadde I levere wedde no wyf to-yeere!'

'Abyde!' quod she, 'my tale is nat bigonne.

Nay, thou shalt drynken of another tonne,   170

Er that I go, shal savoure wors than ale.

And whan that I have toold thee forth my tale

Of tribulacion in mariage,

Of which I am expert in al myn age –

This is to seyn, myself have been the whippe –

Than maystow chese wheither thou wolt sippe

Of thilke tonne that I shal abroche.

Be war of it, er thou to ny approche;

For I shal telle ensamples mo than ten.

"Whoso that nyl be war by othere men,   180

By hym shul othere men corrected be."

The same wordes writeth Ptholomee;

Rede in his Almageste, and take it there.'

'Dame, I wolde praye yow, if youre wyl it were,'

165–70: What] *why*   bye it on] *pay-it with*   to-yeere] *this year*   Abyde!] *Hold on!*   tonne] *barrel*

171–80: savoure] *taste*   abroche] *open*   nyl] *will not*   war] *instructed*

181–4: By hym] *by his example*]   Ptholomee] *Ptolemy*

Seyde this Pardoner, 'as ye bigan,
Telle forth youre tale, spareth for no man,
And teche us yonge men of youre praktike.'
'Gladly,' quod she, 'sith it may yow like;
But yet I praye to al this compaignye,
If that I speke after my fantasye,   190
As taketh not agrief of that I seye,
For myn entente nys but for to pleye . . .

'My fourthe housbonde was a revelour –
This is to seyn, he hadde a paramour –
And I was yong and ful of ragerye,
Stibourn and strong, and joly as a pye.
How koude I daunce to an harpe smale,
And synge, ywis, as any nyghtyngale,
Whan I had dronke a draughte of sweete wyn!
Metellius, the foule cherl, the swyn,   460
That with a staf birafte his wyf hir lyf
For she drank wyn, thogh I hadde been his wyf,
He sholde nat han daunted me fro drynke!

185–90: praktike] *experience*   fantasye] *whim*
191–2: agrief] *amiss*   pleye] *joke*
453–60: revelour] *man-about-town*   paramour] *mistress*   ragerye] *sexual
impulses*   Stibourn] *stubborn*   pye] *magpie*
461–3: For] *because*   daunted] *scared*

And after wyn on Venus moste I thynke,
For al so siker as cold engendreth hayl,
A likerous mouth moste han a likerous tayl.
In wommen vinolent is no defence –
This knowen lecchours by experience.
But – Lord Crist! – whan that it remembreth me
Upon my yowthe, and on my jolitee,   470
It tikleth me aboute myn herte roote.
Unto this day it dooth myn herte boote
That I have had my world as in my tyme.
But age, allas, that al wole envenyme,
Hath me biraft my beautee and my pith.
Lat go. Farewel! The devel go therwith!
The flour is goon; ther is namoore to telle;
The bren, as I best kan, now moste I selle;
But yet to be right myrie wol I fonde.
Now wol I tellen of my fourthe housbonde.   480

The Pardoner's Tale

The Pardoner is one of the great self-confessed villains in literature,
developed from the allegorical figure 'Faux Semblant' ('False

464–70: likerous] *lecherous*   tayl] *nether region*   vinolent] *drunkenness*
471–80: boote] *good*   envenyme] *poison*   pith] *vigour*   bren] *chaff*   fonde]
attempt

Seeming') in the *Roman de la Rose*, and more brazen that Iago or Edmund. He tells the pilgrims he is a scheming charlatan who makes his money by deploying false relics – pillow-cases and pigs' bones – as he goes around selling indulgences. But he is such a brilliant preacher, he says, that he can persuade people of what he says even after telling them he is lying. This extract starts at the point (line 663) where he picks up again his chilling tale of the encounter of three young criminals with Death. It has often been saluted as the first great short story in English, driving to its grim end with a spare inevitability. This extract begins at line 660, at the end of the Pardoner's Prologue.

> But, sires, now wol I telle forth my tale.
> Thise riotoures thre of which I telle,
> Longe erst er prime rong of any belle,
> Were set hem in a taverne for to drynke,
> And as they sat, they herde a belle clynke
> Biforn a cors, was caried to his grave.
> That oon of hem gan callen to his knave –
> 'Go bet', quod he, 'and axe redily
> What cors is this that passeth heer forby;
> And looke that thou reporte his name weel.'   10

1–10: telle forth] *get on with telling*   erst er prime] *before 6 a.m.*   set hem] *settled in*   clynke] *ring*   cors] *corpse (which)*   Go bet] *go quickly*   axe redily] *ask immediately*   forby] *nearby*

'Sire', quod this boy, 'it nedeth never-a-deel;
It was me toold er ye cam heer two houres.
He was, pardee, an old felawe of youres;
And sodeynly he was yslayn to-nyght,
Fordronke, as he sat on his bench upright.
Ther can a privee theef men clepeth Deeth,
That in this contree al the peple sleth,
And with his spere he smoot his herte atwo,
And wente his wey withouten wordes mo.
He hath a thousand slayn this pestilence.   20
And, Maister, er ye come in his presence.
Me thynketh that it were necessarie
For to be war of swich an adversarie.
Beth redy for to meete hym everemoore;
Thus taughte me my dame; I sey namoore.'
'By seinte marie!', seyde this taverner,
'The child seith sooth, for he hath slayn this yeer,
Henne over a mile, withinne a greet village,
Bothe man and womman, child, and hyne, and page;

11–20: it nedeth never-a-deel] *I don't need to*   pardee] *by God*   felawe]
comrade   yslayn] *killed*   Fordronke] *blind drunk*   privee] *stealthy*   clepeth]
call   sleth] *kills*   smoot] *struck*   atwo] *in two*   this pestilence] *during this
plague*
21–9: Maister] *Sir*   everemoore] *always*   dame] *mother*   taverner]
landlord   seith sooth] *is right*   Henne over a mile] *within a mile of here*
hyne] *servants*

189

I trowe his habitacioun be there.   30

To been avysed greet wysdom it were,

Er that he dide a man a dishonour.'

'Ye, Goddes armes!' quod this riotour,

'Is it swich peril with hym for to meete?

I shal hym seke by wey and ek by strete,

I make avow to Goddes digne bones!

Herkneth, felawes, we thre been al ones;

Lat ech of us holde up his hand til oother,

And ech of us bicomen otheres brother.

And we wol sleen this false traytour Deeth.   40

He shal be slayn, he that so manye sleeth,

By goddes dignitee, er it be nyght!'

Togidres han thise thre hir trouthes plight

To lyve and dyen ech of hem for oother,

As though he were his owene ybore brother.

And up they stirte, al dronken in this rage,

And forth they goon towardes that village

Of which the taverner hadde spoke biforn.

And many a grisly ooth thanne han they sworn,

30: habitacioun] *dwelling-place*
31–40: avysed] *forewarned*   a dishonour] *some mischief*   to Goddes digne] *by God's sainted*   al ones] *of one mind*   til oother] *to each other*   bicomen] *become*   sleen] *kill*
41–9: er] *before*   hir trouthes plight] *sworn their agreement*   ybore] *born*
stirte] *jump*   grisly] *savage*

And Cristes blessed body al torente –   50
'Deeth shal be deed', if that they may hym hente!
Whan they han goon nat fully half a mile,
Right as they wolde han troden over a stile,
An oold man and a povre with hem mette.
This olde man ful mekely hem grette,
And seyde thus 'Now, lordes, God yow see!'
The proudeste of thise riotoures three
Answerde again 'What, carl, with sory grace!
Why artow al forwrapped save thy face?
Why lyvestow so longe in so greet age?'   60
This olde man gan looke in his visage,
And seyde thus: 'For I ne kan nat fynde
A man, though that I walked into Ynde,
Neither in citee ne in no village,
That wolde chaunge his youthe for myn age;
And therfore moot I han myn age stille,
As longe tyme as it is Goddes wille.
Ne Deeth, allas! ne wol nat han my lyf.
Thus walke I, lyk a restelees kaitif,

50: torente] *torn*
51–60: hym hente] *get hold of him*   Right] *just*   troden] *climbed*   povre]
poor   mekely] *modestly*   yow see] *look after you*   with sory grace] *bad luck to
you*   forwrapped] *wrapped up*   save] *except*   Why lyvestow so longe] *How
come you're still alive*
61–9: For] *because*   into Ynde] *as far as India*   han] *keep*   han] *accept*
kaitif] *wretch*

And on the ground, which is my moodres gate,   70
I knokke with my staf, bothe erly and late,
And seye "Leeve mooder, leet me in!
Lo how I vanysshe, flessh, and blood, and skyn!
Allas! whan shul my bones been at reste?
Mooder, with yow wolde I chaunge my cheste
That in my chambre longe tyme hath be,
Ye, for an heyre clowt to wrappe in me!"
But yet to me she wol nat do that grace,
For which ful pale and welked is my face.
But, sires, to yow it is no curteisye   80
To speken to an old man vileynye,
But he trespasse in word, or elles in dede.
In hooly writ ye may yourself wel rede –
"Agayns an oold man, hoor upon his heed,
Ye sholde arise"; wherfore I yeve yow reed,
Ne dooth unto an oold man noon harm now,
Namoore than that ye wolde men did to yow
In age, if that ye so longe abyde.
And God be with yow, where ye go or ryde!

70: gate] *entrance*
71–80: vanysshe] *waste away*   cheste] *treasure-chest*   heyre clowt] *hair shirt*   welked] *withered*
81–9: vileynye] *rudeness*   But he trespasse] *except if he offends*   Agayns] *in the presence of*   hoor] *grey*   arise] *stand up*   yeve yow reed] *advise*   abyde] *live*

I moot go thider as I have to go.'   90
'Nay, olde cherl, by God, thou shalt not so,'
Seyde this oother hasardour anon;
'Thou partest nat so lightly, by Seint John
Thou spak right now of thilke traytour deeth,
That in this contree alle oure freendes sleeth.
Have heer my trouthe, as thou art his espye,
Telle where he is, or thou shalt it abye,
By God, and by the Hooly Sacrement!
For soothly thou art oon of his assent
To sleen us yonge folk, thou false theef!'   100
'Now, sires', quod he, 'if that yow be so leef
To fynde deeth, turne up this croked wey,
For in that grove I lafte hym, by my fey,
Under a tree, and there he wole abyde;
Noght for youre boost he wole him no thyng hyde.
Se ye that ook? Right there ye shal hym fynde.
God save yow, that boghte agayn mankynde,
And yow amende!' Thus seyde this olde man;
And everich of thise riotoures ran
Til he cam to that tree, and ther they founde   110

90: thider as I have to] *where I must*
91–100: espye] *spy*   abye] *regret*   assent] *accord*
101–10: leef] *keen*   wole abyde] *will wait*   boost] *bragging*   boghte] *redeemed*
amende] *cure*

Of floryns fyne of gold ycoyned rounde
Wel ny an eighte busshels, as hem thoughte.
No lenger thanne after deeth they soughte,
But ech of hem so glad was of that sighte,
For that the floryns been so faire and brighte,
That doun they sette hem by this precious hoord.
The worste of hem, he spak the firste word.
'Bretheren', quod he, 'Taak kep what that I seye;
My wit is greet, though that I bourde and pleye.
This tresor hath Fortune unto us yiven,   120
In myrthe and joliftee oure lyf to lyven,
And lightly as it comth, so wol we spende.
Ey! Goddes precious dignitee! who wende
To-day that we sholde han so fair a grace?
But myghte this gold be caried fro this place
Hoom to myn hous, or elles unto youres –
For wel ye woot that al this gold is oures –
Thanne were we in heigh felicitee.
But trewely, by daye it may nat bee.
Men wolde seyn that we were theves stronge,   130

111–20: floryns] *florins*   ycoyned] *minted*   Taak kep] *take heed*
wit] *intelligence*   bourde] *fool around*
121–30: joliftee] *jollity*   lightly] *easily*   who wende] *who'd have thought*
felicitee] *happiness*   theves stronge] *clear thieves*

And for oure owene tresor doon us honge.
This tresor moste ycaried be by nyghte
As wisely and as slyly as it myghte.
Wherfore I rede that cut among us alle
Be drawe, and lat se wher the cut wol falle;
And he that hath the cut with herte blithe
Shal renne to the toun, and that ful swithe,
And brynge us breed and wyn ful prively.
And two of us shul kepen subtilly
This tresor wel; and if he wol nat tarie,   140
Whan it is nyght, we wol this tresor carie,
By oon assent, where as us thynketh best.'
That oon of hem the cut broghte in his fest,
And bad hem drawe, and looke where it wol falle;
And it fil on the yongeste of hem alle,
And forth toward the toun he wente anon.
And also soone as that he was gon,
That oon of hem spak thus unto that oother –
'Thou knowest wel tho art my sworen brother;
Thy profit wol I telle thee anon.   150

131–40: doon us honge] *have us hanged*   cut] *lots*   ful swithe] *very quickly*
subtilly] *guardedly*
141–50: cut] *lots*   fest] *hand*   it fil on] *the lot fell*   also soone as] *as soon as*
profit] *advantage*

Thou woost wel that oure felawe is agon.

And heere is gold, and that ful greet plentee,

That shal departed been among us thre.

But nathelees, if I kan shape it so

That it departed were among us two,

Hadde I nat doon a freendes torn to thee?'

That oother answerde, 'I noot hou that may be.

He woot wel that the gold is with us tweye;

What shal we doon? what shal we to hym seye?'

'Shal it be conseil?' seyde the firste shrewe,   160

'And I shal tellen in a wordes fewe

What we shal doon, and brynge it wel aboute.'

'I graunte', quod that oother, 'Out of doute,

That, by my trouthe, I wol thee nat biwreye.'

'Now', quod the firste, 'Thou woost wel we be tweye;

And two of us shul strenger be than oon.

Looke whan that he is set, that right anoon

Arys as though thou woldest with hym pleye,

And I shal ryve hym thurgh the sydes tweye

Whil that thou strogelest with hym as in game,   170

151–60: woost] *know*   departed] *divided*   shape] *organise*   a freendes torn] *a friendly act*   I noot] *I don't know*   woot] *knows*   conseil] *a secret*   shrewe] *villain*

161–70: graunte] *accept*   Out of doute] *of course*   biwreye] *reveal*   we be tweye] *there are two of us*   set] *ready*   ryve] *stab*   tweye] *two*   strogelest] *struggle*

And with thy daggere looke thou do the same;
And thanne shal al this gold departed be,
My deere freend, bitwixen me and thee.
Thanne may we bothe oure lustes all fulfille,
And pleye at dees right at oure owene wille.'
And thus acorded been thise shrewes tweye
To sleen the thridde, as ye han herd me seye.
This yongeste, which that wente to the toun,
Ful ofte in herte he rolleth up and doun
The beautee of thise floryns newe and brighte.   180
'O lord!' quod he, 'If so were that I myghte
Have al this tresor to myself allone,
Ther is no man that lyveth under the trone
Of God that sholde lyve so murye as I!'
And atte laste the Feend, oure enemy,
Putte in his thought that he sholde poysen beye,
With which he myghte sleen his felawes tweye;
For-why the Feend foond hym in swich lyvynge
That he hadde leve him to sorwe brynge.
For this was outrely his fulle entente,   190

171–80: lustes] *desires*   dees] *dice*   acorded] *in agreement*   rolleth] *considers*
181–90: the trone] *the throne*   Feend] *Devil*   beye] *buy*   lyvynge] *way of life*
leve] *permission (from God)*   outrely] *fully*

To sleen hem bothe, and nevere to repente.

And forth he gooth, no lenger wolde he tarie,

Into the toun, unto a pothecarie,

And preyde hym that he hym wolde selle

Som poyson, that he myghte his rattes quelle;

And ek ther was a polcat in his hawe,

That, as he seyde, his capouns hadde yslawe,

And fayn he wolde wreke hym, if he myghte,

On vermyn that destroyed hym by nyghte.

The pothecarie answered 'And thou shalt have   200

A thyng that, also God my soule save,

In al this world ther is no creature,

That eten or dronken hath of this confiture

Noght but the montance of a corn of whete,

That he ne shal his lif anon forlete;

Ye, sterve he shal, and that in lasse while

Than thou wolt goon a paas nat but a mile,

This poysoun is so strong and violent.'

This cursed man hath in his hond yhent

This poysoun in a box, and sith he ran   210

191–200: pothecarie] *chemist*   his rattes quelle] *kill his rats*   polcat] *weasel*
hawe] *yard*   capouns] *chickens*   wreke hym] *avenge himself*   destroyed] *ruined*
201–10: also God] *as God may*   confiture] *concoction*   montance] *amount*
forlete] *give up*   sterve] *die*   a paas] *at walking pace*   yhent] *taken*   sith] *next*

Into the nexte strete unto a man,
And borwed of hym large botelles thre;
And in the two his poyson poured he;
The thridde he kepte clene for his drynke,
For al the nyght he shoop hym for to swynke
In cariynge of the gold out of that place.
And whan this riotour, with sory grace,
Hadde filled with wyn his grete botels thre,
To his felawes agayn repaireth he.
What nedeth it to sermone of it moore?   220
For right as they hadde cast his deeth bifoore,
Right so they han hym slayn, and that anon.
And whan that this was doon, thus spak that oon:
'Now lat us sitte and drynke, and make us merie,
And afterward we wol his body berie.'
And with that word it happed hym, par cas,
To take the botel ther the poyson was,
And drank, and yaf his felawe drynke also,
For which anon they storven bothe two.

211–20: borwed] *borrowed*   shoop] *intended*   sory grace] *evil purpose*   agayn
repaireth he] *he goes back*   sermone] *preach*
221–9: cast] *planned*   storven] *die*

The Merchant's Prologue

The Merchant – presumably unhappily married himself, at least for
Chaucer's purposes: he tells us grimly that he knows well where his
shoe is pinching him – tells the semi-allegorical story of the old fool
January who marries a beautiful young wife, May. It is a tale familiar
from other places in the Middle Ages, but Chaucer's version is
the most grimly comic. Here, starting at line 1311, the merchant
expatiates with ironic bitterness on the joys of the married man.

> A wyf is goddes yifte verraily;
> Alle othere manere yiftes hardily,
> As londes, rentes, pasture, or commune,
> Or moebles, alle been yiftes of fortune,
> That passen as a shadwe upon a wal.
> But drede nat, if pleynly speke I shal,
> A wyf wol laste, and in thyn hous endure,
> Wel lenger than thee list, paraventure.
> Mariage is a ful greet sacrement.
> He which that hath no wyf, I holde hym shent;   10
> He lyveth helplees and al desolat, –
> I speke of folk in seculer estaat.

1–10: yifte] *gift*   verraily] *certainly*   hardily] *definitely*   commune] *lands held
in common*   moebles] *property*   drede nat] *do not doubt*   thee list] *you want*
greet] *powerful*   shent] *ruined*
11–12: seculer estaat] *non-clerical orders*

And herke why, I sey nat this for noght,
That womman is for mannes helpe ywroght.
The hye god, whan he hadde Adam maked,
And saugh him al allone, bely-naked,
God of his grete goodnesse seyde than,
'Lat us now make an helpe unto this man
Lyk to hymself'; and thanne he made him Eve.
Heere may ye se, and heerby may ye preve,   20
That wyf is mannes helpe and his confort,
His paradys terrestre, and his disport.
So buxom and so vertuous is she,
They moste nedes lyve in unitee.
O flessh they been, and o fleesh, as I gesse,
Hath but oon herte, in wele and in distresse.
A wyf! a, Seinte Marie, benedicite!
How myghte man han any adversitee
That hath a wyf? Certes, I kan nat seye.
The blisse which that is bitwixe hem tweye   30
Ther may no tonge telle, or herte thynke.
If he be povre, she helpeth hym to swynke;

13–20: bely-naked] *stark naked*   preve] *find proof*
21–30: terrestre] *earthly*   disport] *entertainment*   buxom] *biddable*   o] *one*
wele] *good circumstances*   benedicite!] *Blessings!*   bitwixe hem tweye] *between
the two of them*
31–2: povre] *poor*   swynke] *work*

She kepeth his good, and wasteth never a deel;
Al that hire housbonde lust, hire liketh weel;
She seith nat ones 'Nay', whan he seith 'Ye'.
'Do this', seith he; 'Al redy, sire', seith she.
O blisful ordre of wedlok precious,
Thou art so murye, and ek so vertuous,
And so commended and appreved ek
That every man that halt hym worth a leek,   40
Upon his bare knees oughte al his lyf
Thanken his God that hym hath sent a wyf,
Or elles preye to God hym for to sende
A wyf, to laste unto his lyves ende.
For thanne his lyf is set in sikernesse;
He may nat be deceyved, as I gesse,
So that he werke after his wyves reed.
Thanne may he boldely beren up his heed,
They been so trewe, and therwithal so wyse;
For which, if thou wolt werken as the wyse,   50
Do alwey so as wommen wol thee rede.

33–40: kepeth] *looks after*   lust] *wants*   hire liketh] *pleases her*   Nay] *no*
Ye] *yes*   Al redy, sire] *right away, sir*   murye] *happy*   commended] *tested*
approved] *proven*   halt hym] *thinks himself*
41–50: preye] *pray*   sikernesse] *certainty*   deceyved] *mistaken*   gesse] *think*
So that] *as long as*   reed] *advice*   trewe] *faithful*
51: rede] *advise*

The Nun's Priest, Daun John (we don't know anything about him), tells the Aesopic fable of the fox and cock, a particularly popular fable in the Middle Ages. Into its innocent setting of the poor widow's farmyard, and its modest literary setting, Chaucer contrives to introduce a great deal of heavy disputation, whether for mock-heroic or serious effect has not been agreed. The tale begins with a pastoral evocation of the virtuous poor.

> A povre wydwe, somdeel stape in age
> Was whilom dwellyng in a narwe cotage,
> Biside a grove, stondynge in a dale.
> This wydwe, of which I telle yow my tale,
> Syn thilke day that she was last a wyf,
> In pacience ladde a ful symple lyf,
> For litel was hir catel and hir rente.
> By housbondrie of swich as God hire sente
> She foond hirself and ek hir doghtren two.
> Thre large sowes hadde she, and namo,   10
> Three keen, and ek a sheep that highte Malle.

1–10: stape] *advanced*   foond] *provided for*
11: keen] *cows*   highte] *was called*   Malle] *Molly*

Ful sooty was hire bour and ek hir halle,
In which she eet ful many a sklendre meel.
Of poynaunt sauce hir neded never a deel.
No deyntee morsel passed thurgh hir throte;
Hir diete was accordant to hir cote.
Repleccioun ne made hire nevere sik;
Attempree diete was al hir phisik,
And exercise, and hertes suffisaunce.
The goute lette hire nothyng for to daunce,   20
N' apoplexie shente nat hir heed.
No wyn ne drank she, neither whit ne reed;
Hir bord was served moost with whit and blak, –
Milk and broun breed, in which she foond no lak,
Seynd bacoun, and somtyme an ey or tweye;
For she was, as it were, a maner deye.
A yeerd she hadde, enclosed al aboute
With stikkes, and a drye dych withoute,
In which she hadde a cok, hight Chauntecleer.
In al the land of crowyng nas his peer.   30
His voys was murier than the murie orgon

12–20: bour] *bedroom*   poynaunt] *spicy*   accordant to] *in proportion to*   cote]
cottage   Repleccioun] *overeating*   Attempree] *moderate*   lette] *prevented*
21–30: shente] *damaged*   Seynd] *smoked*   ey] *egg*   deye] *dairywoman*
yeerd] *yard*

On messe-dayes that in the chirche gon.
Wel sikerer was his crowyng in his logge
Than is a clokke or an abbey orlogge.
By nature he knew ech ascencioun
Of the equynoxial in thilke toun;
For whan degrees fiftene weren ascended,
Thanne crew he, that it myghte nat been amended.
His coomb was redder than the fyn coral,
And batailled as it were a castel wal;   40
His byle was blak, and as the jeet it shoon;
Lyk asure were his legges and his toon;
His nayles whitter than the lylye flour,
And lyk the burned gold was his colour.
This gentil cok hadde in his governaunce
Sevene hennes for to doon al his plesaunce,
Whiche were his sustres and his paramours,
And wonder lyk to hym, as of colours;
Of whiche the faireste hewed on hir throte
Was cleped faire damoysele Pertelote.   50
Curteys she was, discreet, and debonaire,

32–40: sikerer] *more reliable*   logge] *house*   orlogge] *clock*   ascencioun / Of
the equynoxial] *division of the hours*   amended] *improved on*   batailled]
crenellated
41–50: byle] *beak*   jeet] *jet*   toon] *toes*   paramours] *concubines*   throte]
neck   cleped] *called*

And compaignable, and bar hyrself so faire,
Syn thilke day that she was seven nyght oold,
That trewely she hath the herte in hoold
Of Chauntecleer, loken in every lith;
He loved hire so that wel was hym therwith.
But swich a joye was it to here hem synge,
Whan that the brighte sonne gan to sprynge,
In sweete accord, 'My lief is faren in londe!'
For thilke tyme, as I have understonde,   60
Beestes and briddes koude speke and synge.
And so bifel that in a dawenynge,
As Chauntecleer among his wyves alle
Sat on his perche, that was in the halle,
And next hym sat this faire Pertelote,
This Chauntecleer gan gronen in his throte,
As man that in his dreem is drecched soore.
And whan that Pertelote thus herde hym roore,
She was agast, and seyde 'Herte deere,
What eyleth yow, to grone in this manere?   70
Ye been a verray sleper; fy! for shame!'

52–60: compaignable] *socially accomplished*   hoold] *thrall*   lith] *limb*   my life
is faren in londe!] *'My love's gone to the countryside' (a surviving song)*
61–70: dawenynge] *sunrise*   drecched] *troubled*
71: verray] *actual*

And he answerde, and seyde thus: 'Madame,
I pray yow that ye take it nat agrief.
By god, me mette I was in swich meschief
Right now, that yet myn herte is soore afright.
Now God', quod he, 'my swevene recche aright,
And kepe my body out of foul prisoun!
Me mette how that I romed up and doun
Withinne our yeerd, wheer as I saugh a beest
Was lyk an hound, and wolde han maad areest   80
Upon my body, and wolde han had me deed.
His colour was bitwixe yelow and reed,
And tipped was his tayl and bothe his eeris
With blak, unlyk the remenant of his heeris;
His snowte smal, with glowynge eyen tweye.
Yet of his look for feere almoost I deye;
This caused me my gronyng, doutelees.'
'Avoy!' quod she, 'fy on yow, hertelees!
Allas!' quod she, 'for, by that God above,
Now han ye lost myn herte and al my love!   90
I kan nat love a coward, by my feith!

72–80: agrief] *amiss*   mette] *dreamed*   recche aright] *interpret positively*
maad areest] *seized*
81–90: heeris] *coat*   Avoy!] *Shame!*   hertelees] *faint-hearted*

For certes, what so any womman seith,
We alle desiren, if it myghte bee,
To han housbondes hardy, wise, and free,
And secree, and no nygard, ne no fool,
Ne hym that is agast of every tool,
Ne noon avauntour, by that God above!
How dorste ye seyn, for shame, unto youre love
That any thyng myghte make yow aferd?
Have ye no mannes herte, and han a berd? 100
Allas! and konne ye been agast of swevenys?
Nothyng, God woot, but vanitee in sweven is.
Swevenes engendren of replecciouns,
And ofte of fume and of complecciouns,
Whan humours been to habundant in a wight.
Certes this dreem, which ye han met to-nyght,
Cometh of the greete superfluytee
Of youre rede colera, pardee,
Which causeth folk to dreden in hir dremes
Of arwes, and of fyr with rede lemes, 110
Of rede beestes, that they wol hem byte,

92–100: what so] *whatever*   free] *noble*   secree] *discreet*   agast] *afraid*   tool]
weapon   avauntour] *boaster*
101–10: agast] *afraid*   vanitee] *emptiness*   replecciouns] *over-eating*
humours] *bodily fluids*   met] *dreamed*   colera] *choler*   lemes] *flames*

Of contek, and of whelpes, grete and lyte;
Right as the humour of malencolie
Causeth ful many a man in sleep to crie
For feere of blake beres, or boles blake,
Or elles blake develes wole hem take.
Of othere humours koude I telle also
That werken many a man sleep ful wo;
But I wol passe as lightly as I kan.
Lo Catoun, which that was so wys a man,   120
Seyde he nat thus, "Ne do no fors of dremes"?
Now sire', quod she, 'whan we flee fro the bemes,
For goddes love, as taak som laxatyf.'

Chauntecleer refuses to take a laxative, ostensibly relying on several classical authorities, but in fact because 'he loves them never a del': he doesn't like them. But, despite his argument for the reliable power of dreams, he ignores his and is snatched by the fox that the dream prophesied. Bedlam ensues: after the wily fox races off with Chaunticleer who has been undone by his vanity, the narrator goes into an expansive rhetorical lament, while the motley household set off in loud pursuit: 'Ha! Ha! the fox!':

112-20: contek] *battle*   whelpes] *dogs*   lyte] *small*   werken] *make*   wo] *badly*
Catoun] *Dionysius Cato, author of the* Distichs, *much invoked as residuaries of proverbial wisdom in the Middle Ages*
121-3: fors] *heed*

O woful hennes, right so criden ye,
As, whan that Nero brende the citee
Of Rome, cryden senatoures wyves
For that hir husbondes losten alle hir lyves:
Withouten gilt this Nero hath hem slayn.
Now wole I turne to my tale agayn.   130
This sely wydwe and ek hir doghtres two
Herden thise hennes crie and maken wo,
And out at dores stirten they anon,
And syen the fox toward the grove gon,
And bar upon his bak the cok away,
And cryden 'Out! Harrow! and Weylaway!
Ha! ha! the fox!' and after hym they ran,
And ek with staves many another man.
Ran Colle oure dogge, and Talbot and Gerland,
And Malkyn, with a dystaf in hir hand;   140
Ran cow and calf, and ek the verray hogges,
So fered for the berkyng of the dogges
And shoutyng of the men and wommen eeke,
They ronne so hem thoughte hir herte breeke.

124–30: criden] *cried out*   brende] *burned*
131–40: sely] *simple*   crie] *screeching*   stirten] *hurry*   syen] *see*   Out!] *Oh no!*
Harrow!] *Damnation!*   Weylaway!] *Alas!*   staves] *sticks*   Colle . . . Talbot and
Gerland] *(typical dogs' names)*   Malkyn] *Molly*   dystaf] *spinning-stick*
141–4: verray hogges] *very pigs*   fered for] *scared by*

They yolleden as feendes doon in helle;
The dokes cryden as men wolde hem quelle.
The gees for feere flowen over the trees;
Out of the hyve cam the swarm of bees.
So hydous was the noyse, a, Benedicitee!
Certes, he Jakke Straw and his meynee   150
Ne made nevere shoutes half so shrille
Whan that they wolden any Flemyng kille,
As thilke day was maad upon the fox.
Of bras they broghten bemes, and of box,
Of horn, of boon, in whiche they blewe and powped,
And therwithal they skriked and they howped.
It semed as that hevene sholde falle.

But the tables are turned by a surprising piece of ingenuity on the part of Chauntecleer who urges the fox to shout insults at the chasing pack. When he does so, the cock escapes by flying up into a tree. So what is the moral? Are we to believe in the prophetic power of dreams? Is this a morality about vanity and baseless pride, or about the wisdom of keeping your mouth shut when you're winning? Is it – as has been suggested somewhat fancifully – an allegory of the fall of man in Eden? Or is it just a 'folye', a silly story

145–50: yolleden] *yelled*   dokes] *ducks*   quelle] *kill*   Benedicitee!] *Bless us all!*
meynee] *company*
151–7: bemes] *trumpets*   box] *wood*   powped] *yelled*   skriked] *shrieked*
howped] *whooped*   hevene] *sky*

about a fox or a cock and hen, like the cock and bull story at the end of *Tristram Shandy*? No, says the narrator at the end (if we are to take him seriously, as he speaks in the same voice and quotes the same text as in the 'Retraction' at the end of the *Tales*):

> Lo, swich it is for to be recchelees
> And necligent, and truste on flaterye.
>   But ye that holden this tale a folye,   160
> As of a fox, or of a cok and hen,
> Taketh the moralite, goode men.
> For Seint Paul seith that al that writen is,
> To oure doctrine it is ywrite, ywis.
> Taketh the fruyt, and lat the chaf be stille.
> Now, goode God, if that it be thy wille,
> As seith my lord, so make us alle goode men
> And brynge us to his heighe blisse! Amen.

The Canon's Yeoman's Prologue and Tale

The last characters to join the cast of the Canterbury pilgrims are the alchemist Canon and his Yeoman. In this passage, starting at section 8, line 554, the Canon comes riding fast to catch up with the party on a hot day.

158–60: reccheless] *reckless*   folye] *silly story*
161–8: doctrine] *instruction*   ywis] *indeed*

Whan ended was the lyf of Seinte Cecile,
Er we hadde riden fully fyve mile,
At Boghtoun under Blee us gan atake
A man that clothed was in clothes blake,
And undernethe he hadde a whyt surplys.
His hakeney, that was al pomely grys,
So swatte that it wonder was to see;
It semed as he had priked miles three.
The hors ek that his Yeman rood upon
So swatte that unnethe myghte it gon.   10
Aboute the peytrel stood the foom ful hye;
He was of foom al flekked as a pye.
A male tweyfoold on his croper lay;
It semed that he caried lite array.
Al light for somer rood this worthy man,
And in myn herte wondren I bigan
What that he was, til that I understood
How that his cloke was sowed to his hood;
For which, whan I hadde longe avysed me,
I demed hym som chanoun for to be.   20

1–10: Seinte Cecile] *St Cecilia (The Second Nun's Tale)*   Er] *before*
Boghtoun under Blee] *Blean Forest*   gan atake] *caught up with*   surplys]
surplice (clerical long gown)   hakeney] *horse*   pomely grys] *dapple-grey*   swatte]
sweated   priked] *spurred on*   unnethe myghte it gon] *it could hardly walk*
11–20: peytrel] *horse-collar*   foom] *foam*   flekked] *spotted*   pye] *magpie*
male tweyfoold] *doubled over bag*   croper] *crupper*   array] *clothes*   sowed]
sewn on   avysed me] *thought about it*   demed] *thought*   chanoun] *Canon*

His hat heeng at his bak doun by a laas,
For he hadde riden moore than trot or paas;
He hadde ay priked lik as he were wood.
A clote-leef he hadde under his hood
For swoot, and for to keep his heed from heete.
But it was joye for to seen hym swete!
His forheed dropped as a stillatorie
Were ful of plantayne and of paritorie.
And whan that he was come, he gan to crye
'God save', quod he, 'this joly compaignye!   30
Faste have I priked', quod he, 'for youre sake,
By cause that I wolde yow atake,
To riden in this myrie compaignye.

In a curious development, the Yeoman takes over the discussion with the pilgrims. As he describes the dubious – and miserable, grey-faced – transactions of the alchemists, the Canon, his 'master' becomes uncomfortable. He tries to silence the Yeoman but the Host will not allow it, so he 'fledde awey for verray sorwe and shame'. Before launching on his tale of the trickery performed by the canons in exploiting the alchemists' strange obsession with gold-making, the Yeoman describes memorably the destructive power of

21–30: heeng] *hung*   laas] *string*   riden] *ridden hard*   paas] *walk*   ay priked] *ridden the whole time*   wood] *crazy*   clote-leef] *burdock-leaf*   For swoot] *against the sweat*   stillatorie] *still*   Were ful of] *that was full of*

their addiction (862ff), in a passage evocative of modern betting addictions.

> A! Nay! Lat be; the philosophres stoon,
> Elixer clept, we sechen faste echoon;
> For hadde we hym, thanne were we siker ynow.
> But unto God of hevene I make avow,
> For al oure craft, whan we han al ydo,
> And al oure sleighte, he wol nat come us to.
> He hath ymaad us spenden muchel good,   40
> For sorwe of which almoost we wexen wood,
> But that good hope crepeth in oure herte,
> Supposynge evere, though we sore smerte,
> To be releeved by hym afterward.
> Swich supposyng and hope is sharp and hard;
> I warne yow wel, it is to seken evere.
> That futur temps hath maad men to dissevere,
> In trust therof, from al that evere they hadde.
> Yet of that art they kan nat wexen sadde,
> For unto hem it is a bitter sweete, –   50

So semeth it – for nadde they but a sheete,
Which that they myghte wrappe hem inne a-nyght,
And a brat to walken inne by daylyght,
They wolde hem selle and spenden on this craft.
They kan nat stynte til no thyng be laft.
And everemoore, where that evere they goon
Men may hem knowe by smel of brymstoon.
For al the world they stynken as a goot;
Hir savour is so rammyssh and so hoot
That though a man from hem a mile be,   60
The savour wole infecte hym, trusteth me.
And thus by smel, and by threedbare array,
If that men liste, this folk they knowe may.
And if a man wole aske hem pryvely
Why they been clothed so unthriftily,
They right anon wol rownen is his ere,
And seyn that if that they espied were,
Men wolde hem slee by cause of hir science.
Lo, thus this folk bitrayen innocence!

51–60: sheete] *sheet*   brat] *rough cloak*   rammyssh] *ram-like*
61–9: infecte] *pollute*   liste] *want*   unthriftily] *poorly*   rownen] *whisper*
bitrayen] *betray*

The Manciple's Tale

The last tale before the Parson's concluding sermon is told by the Manciple, who we know from the *General Prologue* is a shrewd businessman and man of the world. His tale is a 'Just So' type story of how the crow came to be black; but early in it (156ff) he describes how, despite Phebus's uxorious dedication to his wife, she takes a lover, because, like the pet crow, she cannot bear to be constrained.

> This worthy Phebus dooth al that he kan
> To plesen hire, wenynge for swich plesaunce,
> And for his manhede and his governaunce,
> That no man sholde han put hym from hir grace.
> But God it woot, ther may no man embrace
> As to destreyne a thyng which that nature
> Hath natureelly set in a creature.
> Taak any bryd, and put it in a cage,
> And do al thyn entente and thy corage
> To fostre it tendrely with mete and drynke   10
> Of alle deyntees that thou kanst bithynke,
> And keep it al so clenly as thou may,
> Although his cage of gold be never so gay,
> Yet hath this brid, by twenty thousand foold,

1–10: wenynge for] *thinking by* manhede] *good male qualities* grace] *favour* woot] *knows* embrace] *achieve it* destreyne a thyng] *constrain a quality* entente] *endeavour* corage] *inclination*
11–14: clenly] *carefully*

Levere in a forest, that is rude and coold,
Goon ete wormes and swich wrecchednesse.
For evere this brid wol doon his bisynesse
To escape out of his cage, yif he may.
His libertee this brid desireth ay.
Lat take a cat and fostre hym wel with milk   20
And tendre flessh, and make his couche of silk,
And lat hym seen a mous go by the wal,
Anon he weyveth milk and flessh and al,
And every deyntee that is in that hous,
Swich appetit hath he to ete a mous.
Lo heere hath lust his dominacioun,
And appetit fleemeth discrecioun,
A she-wolf hath also a vileyns knyde.
The lewedeste wolf that she may fynde,
Or leest of reputacioun, wol she take,   30
In tyme whan hir lust to han a make.
Alle thise ensamples speke I by thise men
That been untrewe, and nothyng by wommen.
For men han evere a likerous appetit

15–20: Levere] *prefer*   rude] *wild*   wrecchednesse] *foulness*   doon his
bisynesse] *try its hardest*
21–30: flessh] *meat*   couche] *bed*   lat hym seen] *if it sees*   weyveth] *ignores*
dominacioun] *desire*   fleemeth discrecioun] *drives out judgement*   vileyns]
churlish   lewedeste] *most licentious*   reputacioun] *social standing*
31–4: hir lust] *she wants*   nothyng by] *not at all about*   likerous] *lecherous*

On lower thyng to parfourne hire delit
Than on hire wyves, be they never so faire,
Ne nevere so trewe, ne so debonaire.
Flessh is so newefangel, with meschaunce,
That we ne konne in nothyng han plesaunce
That sowneth into vertu any while.   40
This Phebus, which that thoghte upon no gile,
Deceyved was, for al his jolitee.
For under hym another hadde shee,
A man of litel reputacioun,
Nat worth to Phebus in comparisoun.
The moore harm is, it happeth ofte so,
Of which ther cometh muchel harm and wo.
And so bifel, whan Phebus was absent,
His wyf anon hath for hir lemman sent.
Hir lemman? Certes, this is a knavyssh speche!   50
Foryeveth it me, and that I yow biseche.
The wise Plato seith, as ye may rede,
The word moot nede accorde with the dede.
If men shal telle proprely a thing,
The word moot cosyn be to the werkyng.

35–40: lower] *more base*   newefangel] *whimsical*   sowneth] *tends*
41–50: jolitee] *good humour*   under hym] *besides him*   anon] *quickly*
lemman] *lover*   knavyssh] *ignorant*
51–5: cosyn] *related to*   werkyng] *act*

I am a boystous man, right thus seye I,
Ther nys no difference, trewely,
Bitwixe a wyf that is of heigh degree,
If of hir body dishonest she bee,
And a povre wenche, oother than this –   60
If it so be they werke bothe amys –
But that the gentile, in estaat above,
She shal be cleped his 'lady', as in love;
And for that oother is a povre womman,
She shal be cleped his 'wenche' or his 'lemman',
And, God it woot, myn owene deere brother.
Men leyn that oon as lowe as lith that oother.
Right so bitwixe a titlelees tiraunt
And an outlawe, or a theef erraunt,
The same I seye, ther is no difference.   70
To Alisaundre was toold this sentence,
That, for the tirant is of gretter myght,
By force of meynee, for to sleen dounright,
And brennen hous and hoom, and make al playn,
Lo, therfore is he cleped a capitayn;

56–60: boystous] *plain*   dishonest] *dishonourable*
61–70: gentile] *noblewoman*   estaat] *status*   cleped] *called*   lemman] *bird*
leyn] *lay down*   titlelees] *untitled*   erraunt] *outlawed*
71–5: force of meynee] *power of his army*   sleen] *slaughter*   dounright] *utterly*
make al playn] *flatten everything*   capitayn] *leader*

And for the outlawe hath but smal meynee,
And may nat doon so greet an harm as he,
Ne brynge a contree to so greet mescheef,
Men clepen hym an outlawe or a theef.
But, for I am a man noght textueel,   80
I wold noght telle of textes never a deel;
I wol go to my tale, as I bigan.
Whan Phebus wyf had sent for hir lemman,
Anon they wroghten al hir lust volage.

'The Retractions', wherein 'Taketh the makere of this book his leve'

The last of the *Canterbury Tales* is the long prose treatise on
Penitence, told by the pious Parson, which is not much to the
modern taste. It concludes, like some other medieval works, with a
retraction, expressing pious regret for the composition of the tales
that 'sownen into synne' (*tend towards sin*), including the 'lecherous
lays'. But it expresses satisfaction with the more salubrious works,
such as the translation of Boethius.

Now preye I to hem alle that herkne this litel tretys
or rede, that if ther be any thynge in it that liketh hem,

76–80: small meynee] *a small force*   textueel] *lettered*
81–4: telle] *reckon*   never a deel] *not a bit*   wroghten al hir lust volage] *indulged
all their foolish lust*
1–2: herkne] *listen to*   tretys] *treatise*   rede] *read it*   that liketh hem] *that they
like*

that therof they thanken Oure Lord Jhesu Crist, of whom
procedeth al wit and al goodnesse. And if ther be any
thyng that displese hem, I preye hem also that
they arrette it to the defaute of myn unkonnynge,
and nat to my wyl, that wolde ful fayn have seyd bettre
if I hadde had konnynge. For oure Book seith:
'Al that is writen is writen for our doctrine', and that
is myn entente. Wherfore I biseke yow mekely,   10
for the mercy of God, that ye preye for me that Crist have
mercy on me and foryeve me my giltes; and namely of
my translacions and enditynges of worldly vanitees,
the whiche I revoke in my Retracciouns: as is the Book
of Troilus; the Book also of Fame; the Book of the xxv.
ladies; the Book of the Duchesse; the Book of Seint
Valentynes Day of the Parlement of briddes; the Tales
of Counterbury, thilke that sownen into synne; the Book
of the Leoun; and many another book, if they were
in my remembrance, and many a song and many a   20
leccherous lay: that Crist for his grete mercy foryeve
me the synne.

3–10: therof] *for it*   procedeth] *comes*   wit] *intelligence*   arrette] *attribute*
defaute] *defect*   unkonnynge] *ignorance*   that wolde ful fayn] *would have earnestly
wished*   Book] *Bible*   entente] *purpose*   biseke] *beseech*   mekely] *humbly*
11–20: giltes] *sins*   namely] *especially*   enditynges] *writings*   as is] *such as*
sownen] *tend towards*

The Complaint of Chaucer to His Purse

❧

Although Chaucer died before completing his last and most important work, *The Canterbury Tales*, it is likely that even the 'Retraction' at the end of that was not his last work. This 'Complaint to His Purse' has a concluding 'envoy' (letter) apparently addressed to Henry IV as king, so it must have been written close to the poet's death in about 1400. The function of the poem, however seriously or humorously meant, was to appeal to the new king for the renewal of Chaucer's annuity.

> To yow, my purse, and to noon other wight
> Complaine I, for ye be my lady dere.

1–2: wight] *person*

I am so sory now that ye be light,
For certes but if ye make me hevy chere,
Me were as leef be leyd upon my bere,
For which unto your mercy thus I crye:
Beth hevy ageyn or elles mot I dye.

Now voucheth-sauf this day er it be night
That I of yow the blisful soun may here,
Or see your colour lyke the sonne bright   10
That of yelownesse hadde never pere.
Ye be my lyf, ye be myn hertes stere,
Quene of comfort and of good companye,
Beth hevy ageyn or elles mot I dye.

Now, purse that been to me my lyves lyght
And saveour as doun in this worlde here
Out of this toune help me thurgh your might
Sin that ye wole nat been my tresorere
For I am shave as nye as any frere;
But yet I prey unto your curtesye,   20
Beth hevy ageyn or elles mot I dye.

3–7: hevy] *heavy (miserable as well as weighty)*   Me were as leef] *I'd be just as
happy to*   bere] *deathbed*
8–14: voucheth-sauf] *please grant*   soun] *noise (chinking)*   pere] *equal*
stere] *guiding star*
15–21: tresorere] *accountant*   shave as nye] *head-shaved as short*   frere] *friar*

Lenvoy de Chaucer

O conquerour of Brutes Albyoun
Which that by line and free eleccioun
Been verray king, this song to yow I sende,
And ye that mowen alle oure harmes amende
Have minde upon my supplicacioun.